Where We Came Out

ALSO BY GRANVILLE HICKS

The Great Tradition

John Reed: The Making of a Revolutionary

I Like America

Figures of Transition

Small Town

FICTION

The First to Awaken

Only One Storm

Behold Trouble

There Was a Man in Our Town

GRANVILLE HICKS

Where
We Came Out

1954

The Viking Press · New York

For

R.H.C., Jr.,

and the youngest generation

COPYRIGHT 1954 BY GRANVILLE HICKS

FIRST PUBLISHED BY THE VIKING PRESS IN APRIL 1954

PUBLISHED ON THE SAME DAY IN THE DOMINION OF CANADA

BY THE MACMILLAN COMPANY OF CANADA LIMITED

Grateful acknowledgment is made to the following
which published articles included in part in this
book: *Harper's Magazine*, "How Red Was the Red
Decade?," *Commentary*, "How We Live Now in
America," and the *New Leader*, "Liberals, Fake and
Retarded" and "The Great Reversal."

Library of Congress catalog card number: 54-6428

PRINTED IN U.S.A. BY THE VAIL-BALLOU PRESS, INC.

Contents

I.   A Note for the Neighbors   3

II.   The Best-Educated People   16

III.   The Way It Was   31

IV.   The Red Decade   50

V.   The End of an Era   70

VI.   What We Fight   80

VII.   What We Defend   97

VIII.   Shall We Investigate?   111

IX.   People Get Hurt   134

X.   How to Fight Communism   151

XI.   The Liberals Who Haven't Learned   164

XII.   The Great Reversal   176

XIII.   Renegades and Informers   194

XIV.   The Longer Look   207

XV.   The Way We Live Now   221

XVI.   Hope in America   243

Where We Came Out

I

A Note for the Neighbors

One day early in 1953 I left Roxborough to go to Washington to testify before the House Committee on Un-American Activities, which was beginning to hold public hearings on the subject of Communism in education. Although I was appearing as a friendly witness, it was not an experience to which I looked forward. I wasn't worrying about the questions that might be asked me, for I had already testified in a private session and knew what to expect, but it isn't fun, even in the best of circumstances, to stand up and be shot at.

Moreover, there were two reasons why I was troubled about the whole business. In the first place, I would have to give publicly, as I had already given privately, the names of some seven or eight men whom I had known as members of the Communist party when I was a Counselor in American Civilization at Harvard College in 1938–39. Most of these men, I knew, had left the party about the time I did—that is, after Communist Russia and Nazi Germany signed their non-aggression pact in August 1939—and some of them had subsequently had distinguished academic careers. They were bound to be embarrassed, even if nothing worse happened, when headlines heralded the fact that they had once been Communists.

In the second place, I had serious doubts about the usefulness of the two investigations into Communism in education then being carried on, one by the Jenner committee in the Senate, the other by the Velde committee in the House, before which I was appearing. The reasons for these doubts are set forth in detail later in this book, but I can explain them briefly here. Such investigations, it seemed to me, had accomplished very little—something but not much—in the way of hitting at Communists where they needed to be hit. On the other hand, they had tended to exaggerate the extent and influence of Communism and had thus given many people the jitters. Jittery people, I felt, could do a lot of harm to our educational system. There are always men and women who believe that anybody who doesn't agree with them is a Communist, and whenever such persons are turned loose on our colleges and universities, education gets trampled on.

Why, then, was I willing to testify before the committee? To tell the truth, I had no choice. The law gives Congressional investigating committees the power to subpoena witnesses, and if I had disregarded the subpoena I could have gone to jail. Once before the committee, I had to answer questions unless I was willing to claim the protection of the Fifth Amendment on the ground that I would incriminate myself if I answered them. Under the circumstances this would have been ridiculous, for when I belonged to the Communist party, I belonged to it openly. Moreover, as an anti-Communist, I was not opposed on principle to the investigation of Communism; I merely had doubts about the way in which Congressional investigations were conducted and about the results they were able to achieve. The only way in which I could do justice to all my convictions was to speak out and to say what I thought both about Communism and about Congressional investigations.

So I found myself, on the morning of February 25, 1953, in a large hearing room in the old House Office Building in Washington, while a close friend of mine testified on Communism at Harvard fourteen years ago. Behind a long desk on a platform were the nine Congressmen. At a table below the platform, with his back to the members of the committee, was Frank Tavenner, chief counsel, with his assistants beside him. Opposite Mr. Tavenner the witness was seated, facing the committee. Reporters occupied tables nearby. Floodlights had been set up, and television cameras were operating quietly. Newspaper photographers, with flash cameras, crawled in and out, looking for effective shots. The hall, which could have held three or four hundred persons, I suppose, was a little more than half full, and the spectators came and went as duty or inclination moved them.

During most of two days I was a member of the audience, listening to the testimony of three of my former colleagues. Then I testified for an hour or so and was dismissed. I came home to find a six-column headline in the Troy *Record:*

GRANVILLE HICKS ADMITS PAST
RED TIES BEFORE HOUSE PROBE

As if I have ever made a secret of my "Red ties"! Fifteen years earlier, when my appointment at Harvard was announced, I was asked by a reporter whether I was a member of the Communist party, and I of course replied, "Yes." (That was worth only a one-column headline in the *Record.*) Since that time I have been mentioned again and again in the columns of the *Record* as a Communist or an ex-Communist, and I have written a number of letters to the paper in which I have referred to my party affiliations.

Certainly it was not news to my neighbors that I had been a Communist. Those who were living in Roxborough in the late nineteen-thirties knew well enough that I was a member of the party, for, far from trying to conceal the fact, I boasted of it. They knew, too, that I resigned publicly from the party in September 1939. Since that time I have never taken part in any kind of Communist activity, but on the contrary—and this also is a matter of record—have opposed Communism in every possible way. Why, then, all the fuss? Why should I be called to Washington nearly fourteen years after I publicly broke with the Communist party? Why the headlines in the *Record?*

The explanation is obvious: the American people are acutely concerned with Communism at the present time, and have reason to be. To all intents and purposes we are at war with the Soviet Union, and, as I stated before the House committee, every member of the Communist party is actually or potentially a Soviet agent. It would be suicidal for us not to take steps to find out what the Communists in America are doing. We cannot let them steal our secrets or weaken our efforts to hold back Russian aggression.

But we are going to be sorry if we do not learn to make some sharp distinctions. I have said that every member of the Communist party is actually or potentially an agent of the Soviet Union, and I believe this to be true. It does not follow, however, that everybody who ever belonged to the party was part of the Soviet spy ring. I was never a spy, nor was I ever asked to be one, and the majority of ex-Communists, I believe, could say the same thing. Most people who have joined the party were convinced that they were following an ideal. Some few of these have become Soviet agents, but many more have been disillusioned and have left the party.

Sixteen years ago I wrote a little book of Communist propaganda and called it, in all sincerity, *I Like America*. I did like America, and it was natural that I should, for all through the thirties I was able to live the kind of life that I wanted to live. I couldn't help seeing, however, that I was a member of a privileged minority, and I found nothing un-American in desiring for other people, for all people, the privileges I enjoyed.

I believed that there were great evils and injustices in American life, and of course I was right. I believed that these evils could and should be remedied, and I was right in that too. But I was dead wrong in believing that they could be remedied through the agency of the Communist party.

The process of reasoning by which I arrived at this fatally false conclusion will be examined shortly. It will suffice for now to mention my two major blind spots: (1) I refused to see that the Communist party of the United States was completely subservient to the Soviet Union; (2) I would not admit to myself that the Soviet Union was basically and incurably a totalitarian dictatorship.

The behavior of the American Communists in August 1939, when Russia signed the nonaggression pact with Germany, opened my eyes on the first score. In this moment of crisis the leaders of the party could not conceal the fact that their primary function was to defend Russia, no matter what it did. They even made it clear that they had to wait for Russia to tell them in what terms the defense was to be made—had to wait for the Kremlin to give them the new line. This was not the kind of party I thought I had belonged to, and I got out.

On the second point my awakening took a little longer, but the Soviet Union did its best to educate me. The partition of Poland, the seizure of the Baltic Republics, and the war against Finland demonstrated that Communist Russia could be just as aggressive as Nazi Germany, whose aggressiveness all Communists had bitterly denounced before August 23, 1939. I began to think back to some of the unpleasant facts my faith-bound mind had refused to examine—the Moscow trials of the late thirties, for instance. I began to read some of the books that I had dismissed—without reading them—as capitalist propaganda. It did not take me long to conclude that there was no essential difference between Communist tyranny and fascist tyranny.

So I realized that I had been wrong, but that didn't convince me that all the people who had opposed Communism had been one hundred per cent right. I had been wrong, but partly for the right reasons. Other people had been right, but some of them for the wrong reasons. In so far as I had believed that human beings could control economic forces and triumph over economic depression, I had been right. I had been right, too, in my outspoken opposition to fascism. (Today people are sometimes suspected of having had Communist sympathies because they were "prematurely" alarmed about fascism. The suspicion has some practical validity, for the Communists were the first to call attention to the fascist threat, but non-Communists ought to blush when they raise the charge of "premature anti-fascism.") I had been betrayed, in part at any rate, by impulses that I can only regard as essentially generous.

To say this sounds self-righteous, as if I thought of myself as an innocent victim. Perhaps I do, but I know very well that I had no business being either innocent or a victim. Mistakes of judgment are exactly the kind of mistake for which an intellectual [1] cannot be forgiven. Yet, on my own behalf and on behalf of many other ex-Communists, I must insist that a mistake of judgment is not the same thing as a deliberate act of treason. There were many people in the thirties for whom Communism and a love of America did not seem incompatible.

I liked America in 1938, but I like it even better in 1954. For one thing, many of the evils I saw then have been corrected. Our nation is more prosperous than ever before in history, and prosperity is more widely distributed. Though inequities still exist, the majority of working people labor in decent conditions, for reasonable hours, at high pay, while the aged, the sick, and the handicapped are better taken care of than in the past. How our high standard of living has been brought about and whether it can be maintained are questions to be looked into, but that high standard is a reality.

There have been gains in other ways, too. In 1952, for the first time in our history, a year went by without a single lynching. Discrimination against Negroes, though still powerful and evil, has diminished during the past ten years to an

---

[1] An unsatisfactory but unavoidable term—what I mean by it will become clear.

extent that the greatest optimist could not have believed possible. Other types of racial and religious prejudice persist, but
we are on guard against them, and they do less and less harm.
There is nowhere nearly so much injustice as there was
sixteen years ago when I wrote *I Like America*.

On the other hand, there is more and more cause for dis-
liking and distrusting Russian Communism. Not only has its
totalitarian character been intensified during and since the
war; its aggressiveness has become evident to all. Immediately
after the war the Communists took over the governments of
Poland, Yugoslavia, Rumania, Bulgaria, and Albania, and
later those of East Germany, Hungary, and Czechoslovakia.
The technique was always the same: the Communist party,
operating through some kind of popular front, seized power
and eliminated the opposition parties. It then eliminated the
parties allied with it and established an absolute dictatorship. In the so-called satellites we have been able to watch
the unfolding of the Communist pattern: seizure of power,
liquidation of opposition, suppression of every kind of freedom, reorganization of both the government and the economic system on the Soviet model, and finally purges within
the Communist party itself. (In Yugoslavia the purge didn't
work.) The satellites, though nominally independent, are
to all intents and purposes parts of the Soviet Union, and
Russians occupy dominant positions in their industries and
their armies.

Soviet expansion precipitated the third world war, which is
no less a war because it can be called cold. Only resolute
action on the part of the United States saved Greece from
the fate of the other Balkan countries. Only the technological

miracle of the airlift kept West Berlin free. Only a prompt decision and the loss of many lives preserved South Korea. However much Soviet leaders may talk about their desire for peace, they always act on the assumption that war is inevitable, and that is the kind of prediction that is likely to be self-fulfilling.

In this war, cold or hot, I am unreservedly on the side of the United States. Horrible as the prospects of full-scale warfare are and dire as the consequences may be for all the peoples of the world, the fact remains that there would be hope for mankind in a victory of the United States and the West, none at all in the victory of Russia.

All but a handful of Americans, I believe, are agreed that we must resist Russian aggression, but the situation is not so simple as that suggests. What complicates it, of course, is the fact that Russia is the center of what purports to be not a national but an international movement. In every country in the world there are, in varying numbers, people who believe, or profess to believe, that they can serve a great ideal by following the example and accepting the leadership of the Soviet Union. We have such people in the United States, and the big argument today concerns the question of what we should do about them.

These people, these Communists, are, as I have said, actual or potential agents of Soviet Russia, and I believe, as most Americans do, that we cannot permit them to engage in activities that threaten our national security. But some Americans go much further than that: they say that Communism must be uprooted and that every Communist and Communist sympathizer must be exposed and punished. They do not limit themselves to attacking Soviet agents nor even to attacking members of the Communist party; they are out to get everyone who is or ever has been associated even remotely with Communist activities. Some, indeed, go beyond that: they attack those whom they call "Communist-minded." They admit that so-and-so was never a Communist and never had anything to do with Communist fronts, but, they say, he has the kind of mind that makes him naturally sympathetic— "soft" is the word they generally use—toward Communism.

The damage that this heresy-hunting can do—and is doing —to our country and its people is a subject I discuss at length later in this book. What I want to point out here is that it is hurting us in our fight against Soviet aggression, which is our great task. By exaggerating the importance of Communism in America, it prevents us from seeing clearly the terrible problems that confront us throughout the world, and the fear it inspires lowers our morale. Futhermore, the heresy-hunters are trying to shut up, or even to lock up, people who are firmly opposed to the Soviet Union and all that it stands for. It is a fact that the majority of those Americans who have fallen under Communist influence in the past twenty years are now strong anti-Communists; and as for those called "Communist-minded," they are, as a general rule, much better Americans than the heresy-hunters and a good deal closer to the great traditions of the American past. And these are the people whom the heresy-hunters insist on treating as enemies at a time when we need all the resources we can find.

There is another and obvious danger in this heresy-hunting. It aims not merely at getting rid of dangerous people but also at suppressing an idea. Communism as an idea—the idea of political, economic, and social equality—is very ancient. It was given a particular form in the middle of the nineteenth century by Karl Marx, and to the Marxist variety of communism the rulers of the Soviet Union still profess allegiance, even though in practice they have moved in quite a different direction. Communist ideas, whether Plato's or Thomas More's or Marx's or Malenkov's, have to be treated like other ideas: that is, they have to be rationally analyzed, and if they are wrong, their errors have to be pointed out. You may think all communist ideas are vicious, but that doesn't mean that police power should be used against them. The trouble is that when people start suppressing ideas there is no telling where they will stop.

Nor can we assume that the self-appointed crusaders against Communism are merely wrong-headed but well-intentioned zealots. Our folklore has always recognized the principle of guilt by association with its proverbs about birds of a feather, the dog with a bad name, and smoke and fire. A hated man, a hated cause, a hated country is to the practical politician something with which he must associate his opponents if it can possibly be done. Many of the leaders of the anti-Communist crusade are fighting liberalism or progressive education or socialized medicine or the excess profits tax. Some are quite simply making political careers for themselves. Their tactics are familiar enough, but that doesn't mean they aren't dangerous. We soon may be—indeed, history may record that we now are—engaged in fighting for our existence as individuals and as a nation, and we have no ammunition to waste on furthering private prejudices and private ambitions.

Naturally I get into arguments about Communism, and I am sure that some acquaintances think of me as pro-Communist and others as rabidly anti-Communist. I have no patience with people—there are still a few left—who apologize for the Soviet Union, but I am equally impatient with people who regard Senator McCarthy as the savior of the nation. All my experience with Communism convinces me that Soviet Russia is a great danger and that Joe McCarthy's way of combating that danger is not only ineffectual but catastrophic.

That is the reason for my writing this book. It is not a history of Communism, nor an analysis of Communist theory, nor an examination of the record of Communism in Russia and elsewhere. It is in no sense a confession, nor is it the objective study of the impact of Communism on the American intelligentsia that is so badly needed. It is simply a book about Communism in America, about American attitudes toward Communism, and about the kind of life we lead in America today.

I thought I was through with Communism a good many years ago. After I got out of the party, I had to spend some time in re-examining my ideas, in finding out where I, and many others, had gone wrong. When that job was finished to my satisfaction, I turned my attention to other matters. But circumstances—chiefly the aggressiveness of the Soviet Union and secondarily the eagerness of some Americans to turn that aggressiveness to private advantage—have made Communism everybody's business, and if I have something to say on the subject, as I think I have, I ought to say it. Moreover, though I was never guilty of espionage or any other crime against

the government, my conscience isn't clear. How can I tell
how many persons my books, my speeches, or my personal
example may have influenced to join the Communist party?
Some of these persons may still be in the party, may be among
its dangerous members. This is a matter in which I have a
special responsibility.

And, besides, I should like to get the record straight for my
neighbors. We have been working together for a dozen years
and more, and I have made some good friends and some good
enemies, and I am as proud of the one as I am of the other.
But here is an issue that rejoices the enemies and disconcerts
the friends, for—fantastic as it seems—I was less condemned
for being a Communist than I now am for being an ex-
Communist. That is the way the times have changed. So what I
want to do is to say, as honestly as I can, what it meant to be
a Communist in the nineteen-thirties and what I think can
and should be done about Communism today.

But that is not the whole story, for it seems clear to me that
what is going on in America today is important for the whole
world. Here in this little town in which I live I constantly
see evidences of a revolution more significant than the revolution I dreamed of when I was a Communist. And if we are
to win this war, it is as important to understand what we are
fighting for as what we are fighting against.

II

The Best-Educated People

This book grew out of a conversation that took place a few weeks after the headline about my "past Red ties" had appeared in the local paper. As I entered one of the village stores, I was hailed by two men from a nearby town. I had got to know them the preceding fall, when they were working on the library we were building, and we talked about the weather and our familes and how the library was coming along. Then the younger of the men, pretending to be offhand, said, "Did they give you a bad time in Washington?"

"No," I answered, "not really. I think I made out all right."

"I never knew you were mixed up with those guys," he said.

I was surprised. "I thought everybody in Rensselaer County knew," I said.

"I've heard talk," the older man put in, "but I don't believe more'n half of what I hear."

The younger man was looking thoughtful. "What I want to know," he said earnestly, "is how it happened that some of the smartest, best-educated people in the country fell for that gang." He paused and was obviously abashed. "Why, hell, I suppose you belong in that class yourself."

I was grateful to him for thinking of me first as a neighbor and only on a retake as an intellectual. But, so far as academic statistics go, I presumably am one of the best-educated people, and there is no denying that I, along with a certain number of people like me, fell for that gang.

There are men and women, I realize, to whom one can't even begin to explain a thing like that. They have been brought up to believe that their country is right, even, so to speak, when it is wrong. To them communism has always been bad in exactly the same sense that whatever is tabu is bad to a Polynesian—that is, not merely bad but quite literally unthinkable. It is foreign, immoral, irreligious. Whatever word you can think of as damning a thing to hell, communism is it.

But fortunately a lot of people, including many who haven't much formal education, are more discriminating. There is a man in our town, a skilled mechanic, a great hunter, and, as I told him the other day, the most independent cuss I have ever known. He read my *Small Town* when it was published in 1946, and found it, so I was told, rather dry and bloodless. But then he stumbled on *I Like America,* the book that I wrote when I was a Communist and wrote as propaganda for Communism. He is not a man to be frightened by a word, and he felt in the book a genuine concern for working people. He has liked me better since then.

I have another neighbor, also a mechanic, who has been a first-rate friend of mine for twenty years. Because he is my friend, he has been taken for a ride more than once in the factory in which he works. It doesn't bother him in the least. Since he is a Democrat and since the people who ride him are usually Republicans, he has worked out this formula: "Sure, Hicks was wrong, but he had sense enough to admit it, and that's more sense than you'll ever have if you live to be a hundred."

To such people I think I can explain how it happened that for four years and some months I was a member of the Communist party. When I say that I can explain, I don't mean that I can justify. If all anybody wants is for me to admit that I was wrong, I will do so cheerfully, as I have been doing, whenever given the occasion, for the past fourteen years, and expect to go on doing for the rest of my life. But I believe that my friend from the nearby town was sincere when he said that he would like to know how it happened, and it is to people who want to know—not to those who can't wait to cry, "Yah, yah, yah"— that I address myself.

When I appeared before the House Committee on Un-American Activities, Mr. Frank Tavenner, the committee counsel, began with the routine questions. He said, "Will you state for the committee, please, what your formal educational training has been?"

I replied, "I was educated in the public schools of New Hampshire and Massachusetts. I did my undergraduate work at Harvard and was graduated in 1923 with my A.B. degree. From 1923 to 1925 I was at Harvard Theological School. In 1928–29 I was back at Harvard and took my Master's degree in English."

An important part of my life is summed up in those sentences. My father was a white-collar worker, never really prosperous and during much of my boyhood barely able to make both ends meet, but from as far back as I can remember it was taken for granted that I would go to college. I would

have to help myself, of course, but I could count on my parents
to make every possible sacrifice to help me.

My father and mother were solid, conventional, middle-
class citizens. They believed that people should be hard-
working, self-respecting, frugal, and honest. They should live
within their means, keep out of trouble with the law, and stay
on good terms with their neighbors. They should be contented
in whatever circumstances they found themselves, but at the
same time they should encourage their children to get ahead
by honorable means, the most honorable being education.

I was not quite thirteen when the First World War began,
and it became an important educational experience for me.
My father, who as a rule took only a casual interest in current
events, was strongly pro-Allies, and he and I followed with
care the progress of the war. We were delighted when the
United States entered the conflict, and I harangued high-
school assemblies, sold war bonds, and otherwise conducted
myself like the patriotic youth I was. But at the same time,
thanks to the minister of the Universalist Church that we
attended, I was thoroughly indoctrinated in Wilsonian idealism: I believed that an Allied victory not only should but
certainly would bring peace and democracy to the entire
world.

The year after the war ended I entered Harvard, which I
had been told—quite accurately as it turned out—was a poor
boy's college. Youth usually loses some illusions in college;
it is a necessary part of education; but for me and my generation the process of disillusionment was uncommonly rapid
and violent. Those who were a little older lost their illusions

in France or immediately after their return from France, as
some of them were beginning to say in the books they were
writing. We, who were too young to have taken part in the
war, lost ours more quietly but just as completely. The Versailles Treaty was not the kind of peace we had been promised,
and the failure of the United States to join the League of
Nations seemed the betrayal of all our hopes.

We were disillusioned but not exactly unhappy. As we
looked at the world around us, we found a great deal to de-
plore, but it must be admitted that we enjoyed deploring it.
Our spokesmen were constantly saying that the older generation had let us down, and we felt that to be true and very sad,
but we were not unaware of the fact that it gave us a moral
advantage. It was, for many reasons, a period of changing
standards, a period in which the young could defy the old
and get away with it, and that is the kind of period in which
it is fun to be young.

One of the magazines that expressed the post-war mood was
the *Nation,* of which I have more to say later on. Lewis Gan-
nett went to work on the *Nation* in 1919, and a few years ago
he wrote about it in these terms:

> Those were rousing days on Vesey Street. Every week's issue was
> a new adventure. The country was still in a state of war shock: it
> was blockading Germans, seeing reds under every bed, crushing
> strikes in the name of freedom. And yet there was a breeze of hope
> in the air, a stirring all round the world. . . . And there was ex-
> hilaration in fighting the whole wicked world.

John Dos Passos, who had sprung into prominence as a
spokesman for the disillusioned with his novel, *Three Soldiers,*
recognized the ambivalence of the post-war mood when he

wrote an introduction for the Modern Library edition of that book. It was a bitter book, and everybody commented on its bitterness when it was published, but Dos Passos, looking back a dozen years later, knew that it was a hopeful book as well, that hope was what underlay its bitterness, and he wrote of the spring of 1919:

Any spring is a time of overturn, but then Lenin was alive, the Seattle general strike had seemed the beginning of the flood instead of the beginning of the ebb, Americans in Paris were groggy with theatre and painting and music; Picasso was to rebuild the eye, Stravinski was cramming the Russian steppes into our ears, currents of energy seemed breaking out everywhere as young guys climbed out of their uniforms, imperial America was all shiny with the new idea of Ritz, in every direction the countries of the world stretched out starving and angry, ready for anything turbulent and new, whenever you went to the movies you saw Charlie Chaplin.

Something of that excitement came through to a young student whose chief concern was with part-time jobs, marks that would produce scholarships, and other practical considerations, and in my junior year I joined the Harvard Liberal Club. The president that year was an energetic fellow, and whenever he discovered that some prominent dissenter was going to visit Cambridge or Boston, he offered him the hospitality of the clubhouse. In exchange the distinguished guests spoke at lunch, two or three or four of them a week. I listened to anarchists, Communists, Socialists, single-taxers, pacifists, to people who proposed to save the world by birth control or prison reform or workers' education or vegetarianism, to advocates of the Plumb plan, friends of Sacco and Vanzetti, foes of the Versailles Treaty, to admirers of Ramsay MacDonald, disciples of Mahatma Gandhi, enemies of Benito Mussolini. And as if that wasn't enough, I used to go to Ford Hall Forum on Sunday evenings and listen to the same kind of people—often, of course, to the same people.

We who belonged to the Liberal Club were not all intense and serious-minded young men; on the contrary, from the point of view of the Young Communists of a decade later, we were frivolous dilettantes. But we did feel that there was a great deal wrong with the world, and at the same time we were convinced that what was wrong could be remedied. We would listen to anybody who condemned the *status quo* and proposed to change it. That the reforms proposed and the systems expounded were more often than not irreconcilable we had sense enough to realize, but we regarded the will as more important than the scheme, and we felt that somehow all the best features of all the proposals could be combined, when the time was ripe, in one flawless formula for utopia.

Why were we so hostile to the *status quo*? I suppose that each individual's bill of complaints would have had its special features, but in speaking for myself I know I am speaking for some of my contemporaries. In the first place, perhaps because I had missed the war myself, I was deeply affected by the fact that so many men only a little older than I had been killed or injured in a struggle that I now believed to have been un-necessary and futile. War, any war, now had come to seem the greatest of evils, and a system that produced wars could only be bad. In the second place, I had encountered at Harvard sufficient examples of economic inequality to feel that some-thing less than justice prevailed. I wasn't particularly sorry for myself, for I realized that I was enjoying special privileges, but if I, on a budget that allowed for a few luxuries such as second-balcony theater tickets, but only at the expense of desserts, could be considered privileged, most people must be badly off. Finally, and perhaps this is the most important, I had never been able to accept the idea, so generally prevalent, that the most important thing in life was the making of money. A society whose standards were pecuniary was not a society I could respect.

What we meant by the *status quo* included much more than economics and politics. We were attacking an attitude that was embodied in the pronouncements of Warren Gamaliel Harding and Calvin Coolidge, in such books as Bruce Barton's *The Man Nobody Knows,* in the success stories that filled the back pages of the *American Magazine.* Our quarrel was with the Philistines—the Babbitts, as Sinclair Lewis had taught us to call them—and anyone who would smite them was our ally. H. L. Mencken, with his constant and diverting warfare against the "booboisie," was more of a hero in our eyes than, say, Robert LaFollette, for whom most of us voted in 1924. We sympathized with the sober-sided pacifism of Devere Allen and Kirby Page, and we admired Powers Hapgood for casting his lot with the coal miners, but we got more excited about Judge Lindsey's views on companionate marriage and Bertrand Russell's program for sexual freedom. We were impressed by the scholarship and boldness of Charles Beard and Thorstein Veblen, and we used the former's *Economic Interpretation of the Constitution* and the latter's *Theory of the Leisure Class* as ammunition against the enemy, but we also relished the livelier kind of criticism that appeared in such anthologies of dissent as Harold Stearns's *Civilization in the United States*. My own hero in those years was not an American at all but that witty, belligerent, iconoclastic, irrepressible Irishman, George Bernard Shaw.

If the critics of the *status quo* were exceedingly vocal, its supporters were almost inarticulate. There was plenty of flag-waving, plenty of bragging, plenty of abuse for knockers in the *Saturday Evening Post,* the *American,* and other popular magazines, but criticisms were seldom squarely met. In the late twenties, when I was living in western Massachusetts and was on the program committee of a local forum, we looked high and low for somebody who would take the conservative side in a public debate on any one of the controversial issues of the period. Finally a publicist for a large manufacturer of electrical equipment consented to debate with Norman Thomas on public ownership of electric power. Obviously he was accustomed to entertaining Rotarians, Kiwanians, and women's clubs with a pleasant chat on the wonders of electricity, and hadn't realized what he was letting himself in for. As soon as the main speeches were finished, and before there could be rebuttal or questions, he announced that he had to catch a train and fled through the hall, with Mr. Thomas following him to the door and hurling questions after him. Wiser proponents of the *status quo* let prosperity speak for itself, and it spoke loudly enough to drown out talk about Teapot Dome, dollar diplomacy in Central America, the rise of the Ku Klux Klan, the dishonesty of Harding, the ineptness of Coolidge, and other unpleasant aspects of the twenties.

We dissenters were in a curious situation. So far as manners and morals were concerned, the old order was collapsing, not of course because of our attack on it, but because of changed social conditions, especially the increased productivity of industry and the shift of population from country to city. On the other hand, in economics and politics the *status quo* was strongly entrenched and our clamor against it had no effect whatever. This exasperated us, and yet in our hearts we knew we were well off: we had unlimited freedom of criticism and no responsibility.

As I have said, anybody who was against the *status quo* seemed to us to be on our side. Hence our united front embraced not only doctrinaire radicals of every school, all kinds of reformers, and an army of crackpots, but also, in spite of the fact that they were for the most part explicitly nonpolitical, the young poets and esthetes, the experimental novelists and playwrights, and the revolutionaries of the word. We were not discriminating, and we made no pretense of being; we asked what a man was against, not what he was for.

We were bound to look with some sympathy on Soviet Russia, if only because the defenders of the *status quo* were so frightened by it and told such outrageous lies about it. There were other reasons as well. Although few of us were socialists in any dogmatic sense of the term, most of us were inclined to believe that the world was moving in the socialist direction, and we felt that Russia's experiment in socialism was worth watching. We knew that the Soviet Union was no utopia, but what we saw of Russian literature and art convinced us that something interesting and important was going on, and we wished the revolution well.

With local Communists we had little contact. The party was small, was largely made up of the foreign-born, and all through the twenties was torn by factional fights. When we did have anything to do with the Communists, we found them uncomfortable allies—intense, dogmatic, intolerant. But they were against the things we were against, and so, from our point of view rather than theirs, they were part of the united front against the *status quo*.

It must be obvious that I am not talking about all educated people. The majority of my Harvard classmates went into business and were perfectly satisfied with the *status quo*. (Their turn to be dissatisfied came with the election of Roosevelt in 1932.) I am thinking of a small but articulate minority, many of them connected with the arts, some journalists, some teachers. Mostly they were concerned with the communication of ideas. They were the people who read—and, frequently, wrote for—the *Dial,* the *Nation,* the *New Republic,* the *American Mercury.* They were, to use an unsatisfactory term, the intelligentsia.

As I have already suggested, there was the political wing of the intelligentsia and there was the esthetic wing. But the esthetes, by and large, were not so unpolitical as they liked to think themselves, as became apparent during the agitation on behalf of Sacco and Vanzetti. As the six-year fight to save the two Italian anarchists, who had been convicted of murder in an atmosphere of hysteria, drew to its dismal close, the literary people were in the forefront of every demonstration. John Dos Passos wrote a pamphlet on the case. Edna St. Vincent Millay wrote letters and articles, and, along with Dos Passos and John Howard Lawson, got herself arrested for "sauntering and loitering" on the streets of Boston. For many years to come the pain and anger of the intelligentsia over the case found expression in poems and plays and novels.

What made the Sacco-Vanzetti case so momentous for the intelligentsia was the demonstration it gave of their impotence. Despite their unanimity and their vehemence, despite the fact that they were in the right, they could do nothing. The issue was the *status quo*, and not only politicians and judges and college presidents but large numbers of ordinary and usually inert citizens were determined to show the trouble-makers who was boss. It is the anguish of helplessness that one hears in the columns that Heywood Broun wrote for the New York *World*, and, when they had cost him his job there, for the *Nation*. Looking back ten years later, John Dos Passos wrote:

they have clubbed us off the streets   they are stronger   they are rich   they hire and fire the politicians the newspapereditors the old judges the small men with reputations the collegepresidents the wardheelers (listen businessmen collegepresidents judges America will not forget her betrayers) they hire the men with guns the uniforms the policecars the patrolwagons

all right you have won   you will kill the brave men our friends tonight

there is nothing left to do   we are beaten

America our nation has been beaten by strangers who have turned our language inside out who have taken the clean words our fathers spoke and made them slimy and foul. . . .

all right we are two nations

In the spring of 1927 I was teaching at Smith College in Northampton, Massachusetts, and some of us decided that a meeting should be held to ask for clemency for Sacco and Vanzetti. This was not one of those meetings, of which I had seen so many, that were attended only by the convinced; the townspeople turned out in large numbers. They listened with polite but resolute skepticism while Professor James Landis of the Harvard Law School presented the reasons for believing that the two men had not been fairly tried. When he had finished, I read the resolution to be sent to Governor Fuller, and, as the local paper said, "Bedlam broke loose." This was what the townspeople had been waiting for, the chance to shout down the resolution, and their spokesmen—politicians, Legionnaires, businessmen—took the floor to argue hotly that Sacco and Vanzetti ought to be electrocuted and that in any case it was none of Northampton's business. The resolution never came to a vote.

When I read Dos Passos's fiery words about "the two nations," I knew that that was what I had felt when our diplomatic little resolution was killed. But what was this other nation? Was it the rich and powerful of the state? Certainly it was. But it was also the doctors, the lawyers, the shopkeepers, the farmers, the workers. It was practically all my neighbors in Northampton except for other members of the college faculty. The battle was between the intellectuals and everybody else.

It was an example of the phenomenon known as the alienation of the intellectuals, a phenomenon that bears on the problem of the Communist leanings of some of the "smartest, best-educated people." This alienation is often condemned as an evil, but in fact it is only partly evil. In so far as the intellectual is isolated because he thinks he is better than other people or just doesn't want to have anything to do with them, isolation is a bad thing and a symptom of a weakness in our cultural life. But to a certain extent the intellectual is inevitably set apart by his function in our society, and that function, however badly it may be performed by particular intellectuals at a particular moment, is important. The function of the intellectual is to say what he thinks.

Most people don't say what they think. As we all recognize, discretion is necessary in diplomacy, politics, business, law, popular journalism, and even family life. It is, in fact, indispensable to the stability of society, which would fall into chaos if everybody spoke his mind. Yet there must always be a way for indiscreet, unpopular ideas to get expressed or stagnation will result. We need men and women who have some degree of detachment, who are not silenced by institutional loyalties, by the necessity of getting votes, or by the desire for wealth.

The last thing that anyone, even an intellectual, can expect is that the intellectuals will always be right. From their point of view it is important that they should be right as often as possible, that they should not be faddish, that they should not disagree for the sake of disagreeing, that they should know what they are talking about. But the important thing from the point of view of society is that they should be free.

In the twenties the majority of the American people accepted the values of a business civilization: they judged a man's worth largely by the amount of money he was able to make, and it seemed to them reasonable that the men who made the most money should have the most to say about how our society was run. The intellectuals, almost without exception, rejected these values. Their criticisms were sometimes petty, and their notions about what ought to be done were sometimes absurd, but on the whole, it seems to me, they were right. In any case, however, whether they were right or wrong, they were a useful antidote to the prevailing smugness.

If it could be proved to me today that Sacco and Vanzetti were guilty, I should still be glad that we acted as we did, for they were suspected of the crime because they were foreigners and radicals and they were found guilty because there was hysteria in the air. Some of the most eminent and, in their personal lives, most honorable men in Massachusetts closed their eyes to the truth about the trial. Respect for law, they told themselves, had to be preserved; the courts of Massachusetts must be supported. Social stability was more important than the lives of two men. But the intellectuals were not pillars of society; they recognized no duty greater than the duty of speaking out, and they spoke as loudly as they could.

Yet it is no light matter for a group of trained, articulate men and women to reject the central values of their society. My argument has been that our criticisms were useful, as stimulants, even when they were wrong. But there is one thing that has to be taken into account: the *status quo* seemed very strong in the twenties. Whatever might be said against our business civilization, it was delivering the goods; the country was prospering. What would happen if prosperity ceased, if millions of people were jobless and hungry? What would we say then? What would we do? Where would we turn?

III

The Way It Was

The system did collapse, and a certain number of us turned
to Communism. When I talk to college students, I have to
remind myself that they can barely remember Pearl Harbor.
The economic depression of the early thirties, happily for
them, is something they have read about in the history books.
My generation, too, had never experienced a severe depression. Some of us could remember the bad times of 1907—my
father lost a job then—and there had been a brief recession
in 1921. But during most of our years the economic system
had been expanding, and we had come to manhood in the
great boom.

Then it hit us. At first it was merely a stock-market panic,
affecting the rich and the would-be rich. Some of my friends
—professors, doctors, lawyers, people like that—had been
gambling, and they got cleaned out, but they weren't ruined,
since they had their jobs. Most of us weren't affected at all.
But in 1930 employment began to decline, and the decline
went on in 1931 and 1932, until nearly one-third of the nation's working force was idle. Because prices were going down
all the time, those of us who had regular incomes were better
off, but that was small consolation, since we had relatives and
friends who were jobless, and in any case we had eyes. We

could see the Hoovervilles along the railroad tracks outside
any good-sized city—scores or hundreds of shacks made out of
tin and packing boxes and tarpaper, where whole families
were living because they had nowhere else to live. In New
York City, if we were taking the subway late at night, we
stumbled over men sleeping on and under newspapers in the
entrances. Everywhere we went there were bitter-eyed men
and women standing around doing nothing. By the end of
1932 millions of Americans were badly housed, badly clothed,
and badly fed, while factories stood idle and food was dumped
into the ocean.

We had had a low opinion of the system when it worked,
and we could not be expected to think well of it when it proved
a failure. Edmund Wilson recently wrote about the early
thirties:

The slump began, and, as conditions grew worse and worse and
President Hoover, unable to grasp what had happened, made no
effort to deal with the breakdown, a darkness seemed to descend.
Yet, to the writers and artists of my generation who had grown up
in the Big Business era and had always resented its crowding-out
of everything they cared about, these years were not depressing
but stimulating. One couldn't help being exhilarated at the sudden unexpected collapse of that stupid gigantic fraud. It gave us
a new sense of freedom; and it gave us a new sense of power to
find ourselves carrying on while the bankers for a change were
taking a beating.

We were exhilarated, but we were also scared. We had
curiously examined a hundred schemes for the improvement
of society and at our leisure had debated their merits, but we
hadn't had to do anything about them. We had found a thou-

sand flaws in the *status quo,* but we hadn't really expected it
to crumble. Now we had to act and act quickly. Just as, a few
years earlier, we had felt that we had to act to save Sacco and
Vanzetti, so now it was clear to us that we must do something,
make some kind of effort, to put an end to all this misery.

Because we had never liked the Big Business system, and
because the desperate situation called for drastic action, we
were readily convinced that what was needed was a fundamental change in the economic organization of the country.
During the twenties we had listened to the theories of the
Socialists and Communists, but with no more attention than
we had listened to vegetarians and single-taxers. Now, however, we began to take seriously the assertion, made by both
groups, that the only way to end depressions was to socialize
the means of production.

In the twenties we had found the party Socialists more
congenial than the party Communists: they were reasonable,
they spoke our language. But in the crisis their reasonableness
seemed a liability. They had some good ideas but—or so we
believed—no concrete program for putting them into practice. The Communists, on the other hand, could point to the
Russian Revolution of 1917 as an example of the application
of Marxist theories. Led by Lenin, a small group of Marxist
Socialists—called Bolsheviks and later Communists—had actually taken power and had proceeded to socialize the means
of production. It was true that the revolution had been bloody,
that there were no civil liberties in Russia, that the government was a dictatorship; but it was also true that there was no
unemployment in Russia.

As I have said, we had been generally friendly toward

Soviet Russia in the twenties, deploring the crudeness and the excesses of the Bolsheviks but hopeful for the future. It had seemed perfectly impossible, however, that what had happened in backward Czarist Russia could ever happen in prosperous America, even if it were desirable that it should happen, which we doubted. But after 1929 the United States was no longer prosperous and strong; it was poor and hungry and weak. Maybe, we began to say to ourselves, the Communists had something after all.

Early in 1931 Edmund Wilson published an article that showed which way the wind was blowing. "In the abyss of bankruptcy and starvation into which the country has fallen," he wrote, "and with no sign of any political leadership which will be able to pull us out, liberalism seems to have little to offer. I believe," he concluded, "that if the American radicals and progressives who repudiate the Marxian dogma and the strategy of the Communist party hope to accomplish anything valuable, they must take communism away from the Communists, and take it without ambiguities or reservations, asserting emphatically that their ultimate goal is the ownership of the means of production by the government and an industrial rather than a regional representation."

"Take communism away from the Communists!" It was an appealing slogan in those days, but scarcely a practical one. If you really wanted communism, the practical thing was to work with the Communists, who, if they were not numerous, were well organized and active. Wilson himself came to that conclusion, and in the autumn of 1932 he signed a manifesto on behalf of Foster and Ford, the Communist candidates in the national election.

There were many well-known names signed to that manifesto, and some, like my own, not so well-known. It began: "There is only one issue in the present election. Call it hard times, unemployment, the farm problem, the world crisis, or call it simply hunger—whatever name we use, the issue is the same. What do the major political parties propose to do about it?" After saying that the Republican and Democratic parties had no serious proposals and describing the Socialist party as "the third party of capitalism," the manifesto continued: "The Communist Party stands for a Socialism of deeds, not of words. . . . The Communist Party is the only party which has stood in the forefront of the major struggle of the workers against capitalism and the capitalist state. . . . The Communist Party proposes as the real solution of the present crisis the overthrow of the system which is responsible for all crises."

A socialism of deeds, not of words, was what we were looking for, and it was true that the Communists were active in every strike and every unemployment demonstration and that they were being beaten and jailed and sometimes killed. By comparison the Socialists seemed tame and ineffectual. "Becoming a Socialist right now," John Dos Passos wrote in the summer of 1932, "would have just about the same effect on anybody as drinking a bottle of near-beer." Another novelist, Sherwood Anderson, said more soberly, "The artist would also like to think of himself as ready to die for what he believes."

The man who summed it all up was Lincoln Steffens, who had been famous in the early part of the century for his exposures of corruption in government and who had just made a new reputation for himself with the publication of his *Autobiography* in 1931. "I had come to regard the New Capitalism as an experiment," he wrote, "till, in 1929, the whole thing went over the top and slid down to an utter collapse. I went to New York to hear the semi-scientific captains of industry say in words and facial expressions that they did not know what had happened or what could be done about it. They did not understand their own experiment. Then—not till then—did I give up, and turned to see what else there was." And what else was there? "Nobody in the world," Steffens wrote, "proposes anything basic and real except the Communists."

What the Communists proposed was to do what had been done in Russia—to take over the government and to socialize the means of production. Those of us who were becoming interested in communism at this time did not believe that Russia was an earthly paradise, but we did believe that, when you took into account the backwardness of the country, communism had done very well. After all, as we kept reminding ourselves, there was no unemployment in Russia, whereas there was plenty in the United States and in the other capitalist countries, and that proved the superiority of a planned socialist economy to an anarchic capitalist economy. Most of us did not suppose that the revolution in America could or should follow exactly the same course as the Russian Revolution, but we did believe that the same results should be achieved.

What impressed us about American Communists was their absolute devotion to the cause. We didn't like them very well, but they did get results. A friend of mine wrote me at the time: "It is a bad world in which we live, and so even the revolutionary movement is anything but what (poetically and philosophically speaking) it 'ought' to be: God knows, I realize this, as you do, and God knows it makes my heart sick at times: from one angle, it seems nothing but grime and stink and sweat and obscene noises and the language of the beasts. But surely this is what *history* is. It just is not made by gentlemen and scholars, and 'made' only in the bad sense by the Norman Thomases and the Devere Allens and the John Deweys. Lenin must have been (from a conceivable point of view) a dreadful man; so must John Brown, and Cromwell, and Marat, and Stenka Razin, and Mahomet, and all the others who have destroyed and built up. So will our contemporaries in the American movement be. I believe we can spare ourselves a great deal of pain and disenchantment and even worse (treachery to ourselves) if we discipline ourselves to accept proletarian and revolutionary leaders and even theorists for what they are and must be: grim fighters in about the most dreadful and desperate struggle in all history—*not* reasonable and 'critically minded' and forbearing and infinitely far-seeing men. My fundamental conviction about the whole thing, at this stage, is that everything gives way before the terrible social conflict itself: that the power of imperialism must be fought at every turn at every moment with any weapon and without quarter; that the consciousness of the proletariat—its sense of power and its anger—must be built up by every possible device; and that, meanwhile, the kinds of things we are interested in must take their place, where they belong, out of the thickest dust and along the rim of the arena. Let's salvage as much as we can of the rather abstract things we care for, but, golly, let's realize that there are far more basic and primitive things that have to be taken care of first (as long as men are starving and exploited), and do absolutely nothing, at any moment, to impede the work of the men who are fighting what is really our battle *for us*."

If this statement seems high-pitched and even hysterical now, it didn't seem so in 1932, when plenty of people were quite literally starving and the government appeared to be either indifferent or powerless. Many of us, no longer satisfied with a vague, second-hand knowledge of Marxism, had taken to reading Marx and Engels and Lenin, and we were dazzled by the revelation we found in their works. Marx and Engels not only explained the crisis of capitalism; they set forth the laws of history. History, they said, had been made up of a series of class struggles, and now the working class, the proletariat, was struggling against the bourgeoisie. When the proletariat won, as it was bound to do because of the contradictions of capitalism, there would be no class for it to exploit, and therefore it would inevitably establish the classless society—the good society of which utopians long had dreamed. By giving us the key to history, we were convinced, Marxism enabled us to understand science, literature, art, all human activity, and we eagerly launched upon Marxist studies of this, that, and the other thing.

As for Lenin, he had crowned the labors of Marx and Engels by devising the instrument by which the proletarian triumph could be achieved. Out of the necessities of the struggle against Czarist tyranny he had forged a concept of a disciplined, con-spiratorial revolutionary party, and had put it into practice. He had built a party of professional revolutionaries, men and women absolutely committed to revolution and thoroughly trained in methods of bringing it about. His kind of party had triumphed in Russia, and there was, we believed, no reason why it should not triumph throughout the world.

But the exaltation of the early moments of conversion could not last. For one thing, the economic situation began to improve after the inauguration of Roosevelt. The Communist party said, and many of us believed, that the New Deal was merely a stopgap, but we realized that, for the time being at any rate, the revolutionary crisis had passed. Some of the intellectuals who had been so ardent in 1932 lost interest and became nonpolitical. Others went through various phases of disillusionment with the Communist party, many of them allying themselves, at least for a time, with the followers of Leon Trotsky, who proclaimed that they were the true Communists and were bitterly critical of Stalin and the official party. Others substituted workaday cooperation with the Communist party for the heroic ecstasies of the great awakening.

It was in the third group that I was to be found. I joined several Communist fronts, and in 1934 I became an editor of the *New Masses,* the Communist weekly. But I did not join the party. Before 1935 the party made no very strenuous efforts to recruit the intellectuals, and the intellectuals, even though they were willing to work with it, were not inclined to join. However firmly we believed in the principles of communism, we could not help being dubious about the methods employed by the party in the United States. The members were zealots, and from our point of view that was all to the good, but they didn't seem to understand American conditions. They acted as if the United States in 1933 were exactly like Russia in 1917, which struck us as a ridiculous and dangerous assumption. I was enough of an optimist to tell myself that the party leaders were bound to realize their mistakes sooner or later, but meanwhile I was inclined to cooperate only on my own terms.

By the time I did join the party, I had seen evidence of a changed attitude, and soon afterward the change was dramatized by the actions of the Seventh World Congress of the Communist International, held in August 1935. One of the things that had bothered me most about the party's tactics was its failure to cooperate with other groups, especially the Socialist party. The party, it was true, advocated a united front with the Socialists, but at the same time it insisted on describing them as social fascists. In the United States this was important only as a symptom, but in other countries—and especially in Germany, where the Socialists and Communists had been strong enough so that if they had worked together they might have stopped Hitler—it was a calamity. I was therefore delighted when Gorgi Dimitroff, one of the heroes of the struggle against fascism, presented to the Comintern congress a new program for working-class cooperation.

The program as adopted by the Comintern was still on the sectarian side, but the result in the United States was an astonishing liberalization of party tactics. In this country the party did not proceed by formal agreements with other parties and groups but by setting up new organizations and modifying old ones, so that Communists and non-Communists could work together for the aims of what was now called the Popular Front. These aims were primarily resistance to fascism, at home and abroad, the organization of labor unions, and support of New Deal reform measures. Party propaganda lost its Russian coloring and took on a flamboyantly nationalist hue.

"Communism is Twentieth-Century Americanism" was one of the slogans of the later thirties.

The period of the Popular Front was the heyday of Communism in America. Party membership rose to approximately 100,000—it had been 12,000 in 1929—and the party's influence increased proportionally. There were the close fellow travelers, who regularly followed the party line, though for one reason or another they refused to join. There were the more remote fellow travelers, who were willing to cooperate with the Communists for specific causes. And there were the innocents, people who joined the Communist fronts without knowing they were Communist. And all this growth could be attributed to the new tactics adopted in 1935.

It never occurred to me at the time that the new line was really a trick, a device for strengthening Soviet foreign policy. When I joined the party, it was not because I wanted to help Russia, though I had friendly feelings toward the Soviet Union both as an example of working socialism and as the chief enemy of fascism. Nor was it because I desired the overthrow of the government of the United States: toward that government as currently constituted I was sympathetic, both officially as a Communist and in my personal convictions. If a violent revolution came, I believed, it would be led by native fascists, and I would support the government against them (as, in 1936, the Spanish Communists supported the Loyalist government when Franco revolted against it). I joined the party because, as a convinced Marxist, I was in agreement with what I believed to be its ultimate aim—the socialization of the means of production—and especially because it seemed to be leading the struggle against fascism.

Hitler's rise to power had changed not only the strategies of the Kremlin but also the thinking of a great many Americans, including the Communist converts and fellow travelers. According to the Communist International, fascism was "the open terrorist dictatorship of the most reactionary, most chauvinistic, and most imperialistic elements of finance capitalism." We believed that. Fascism to us was a violent expression of the barbarism we had found implicit in a decadent capitalist system, and it was a horrible and immediate menace that must be combated at all costs. It was no accident, we felt, that Hitler, after seizing power, had struck first at the Communists, for they were the leaders everywhere in the fight against fascism. In this country, indeed, it often seemed that they were the only people who understood how dangerous fascism was. In that situation many persons who had previously kept on the sidelines decided to join the party.

Of late there have been attempts to interpret party membership in terms of psychopathology, to say that people become Communists because of personality problems. Of many of the Communists I knew in the thirties this was not true, I think, in any significant way. They were men and women who were doing well in their professions and seemed to be as stable and as happy in their personal lives as the average non-Communist. No one can see all the way through the problem of human motivation, but by and large they appeared to be guided by honest convictions. On the other hand, especially in the period of the Popular Front, the party had more than its share of lost souls. There are always such people about, and at that time the party was the fashionable haven for them. Some were cases from textbooks in psychopathology; others suffered from simpler kinds of frustration—the unsuccessful writers and artists, the sex-starved women, and so on. Many of them had tried other causes before and would try other causes after. Some, indeed, as we ought to have been able to predict then and there, would turn from the most pious kind of Communism to the most rabid kind of anti-Communism.

One thing ought to be clear, and that is that the American Communist party of the Popular Front period was a long way from the Leninist concept of the disciplined, monolithic party of trained revolutionaries. The other day a college student asked me whether joining the party seemed to me at the time an exciting thing to do. It brought, as a matter of fact, a sense of elation, as any difficult and long-postponed decision is bound to do. To a great extent, however, actual party membership was as dull as dishwater. An ordinary meeting of the branch of the party I belonged to in Troy was more like a meeting of the Roxborough Parent-Teacher Association or the Roxborough Volunteer Fire Company than it was like a gathering of conspirators. There were the same tedious harangues, the same wrangles over parliamentary procedures, the same misunderstandings. Such matters as getting new members, raising money, and selling subscriptions to party periodicals always took up a large part of the time. The study period, if there was time for one, was conducted in an atmosphere of perfunctory piety such as one often encounters in the sessions of church societies.

Why, then, did membership in the party seem worth the sacrifices and risks it involved? There were two principal reasons. First, we had the intoxicating sense of being in the mainstream of history that is such a stimulus and such a peril for the convinced Marxist. And, in the second place, we were doing something. While others were questioning and criticizing, we were acting.

What were we doing? For the most part we were working for what seemed to be, and sometimes were, worthy causes. We were calling attention to the dangers of Nazism and trying to help its victims. We were raising money to aid the Loyalists in Spain. We were boycotting and persuading others to boycott Japanese goods. We were helping, so far as we were able, to organize labor unions, in the great wave of unionization that followed the adoption of the National Labor Relations Act. We were soliciting funds for the relief of strikers and holding meetings to denounce the shooting and jailing of strike leaders. We were demanding more adequate relief for the unemployed and more government spending to increase employment.

It is not pleasant to look back now and try to assess the damage we may have done. It is sickening to think that the money we gave and raised for Spain, funneled as it was through party channels, is just as likely to have been used against non-Communist Loyalists as against Franco. Some of the unions we helped to build, remaining under party control, sabotaged American preparations for an anti-fascist war in 1939 and 1940. And even if our efforts had done no harm, they did almost no good, for the party liquidated the whole anti-fascist front, which we had worked so hard to create, after the Communist-Nazi nonaggression pact.

However, I saw no evidence of espionage or sabotage while I was in the party. I believed that these were weapons that should be used in certain circumstances; I would, for example, have used them against a fascist government, as today I would use them against a Communist government. That the circumstances of 1935–39 warranted their use I did not believe. Today, of course, the evidence is overwhelming that all through the thirties the Soviet Union was using American Communists to spy on the American government. I cannot say for sure what I would have done if I had been confronted then with clear evidence of espionage—my faith took some pretty high hurdles—but I think it would have been the end of the party so far as I was concerned.

If I knew nothing about espionage, I knew plenty about the policy of infiltration, and I did not disapprove. I took it for granted that the party would dominate any front it created, and I often helped it to do so. Take, for example, the League of American Writers, most of whose members were not Communists. In discussions held by the party fraction in the League I frequently protested against tactics that seemed to me ineffectual or obvious, but I would have been as shocked as the next one at any suggestion that the party might relinquish its control. I also believed that Communists ought to influence and if possible control whatever labor unions they belonged to. (Why not, since the party's policies were, I believed, right?) Much of the time this was easy to do, for most union members, like most other people, are willing to let somebody else take the responsibility and do the work. In the branch of the Teachers' Union to which I belonged there was no problem at all: party members decided the union's policies in their party meetings, and the non-Communist members —the majority, of course—usually went along without an argument. If necessary, the Communists relied on parliamentary stratagems and whatever political tricks they could work out, but the occasion seldom arose.

At the time the process of infiltration and domination seemed to me natural and reasonable, and it still seems to me that, given the aims of the party—and I mean the avowed aims, not what we now know to be the secret aims—such methods are inevitable. They have, at any rate, been used by many power-seeking organizations besides the party.

If, however, the ethical problem is complicated, the practical problem is not. If anything is certain, it is that non-Communists cannot cooperate with Communists on any terms or for any purpose. Whether it is an organization they have created or one they have moved into, the Communists will run it or they will ruin it. The non-Communists either have to drive the Communists out, if they can, or get out themselves; otherwise they will be used.

This brings us again to the question of party discipline, which, as I have said, was considerably relaxed in the Popular Front period. It is true that I was useful to the party in those days, but I was not the only one who rejected suggestions—they didn't talk much about "directives" at that time—and got away with it. In the Harvard branch we all felt free, within fairly large limits, to disagree with party functionaries. And even in other periods Leninist discipline was an ideal rather than an achievement, for the leaders have never been able to count on the obedience of all the members. Thousands have dropped out whenever there was a change of line, and even in quiet times the turnover in membership is high. When you read that a member of the Communist party is absolutely subject to the will of the party and must do and say whatever the party orders, you are reading about what the party would like to be true rather than what is true. It is therefore dangerous and unfair to assume that because an individual was once a member of the party he was its perfect and willing instrument.

On the other hand, it is foolish to underestimate the power of party discipline. Even in the Popular Front period, when the party had less than complete control, it did exert a powerful influence over its members and was able to get from them most of what it wanted at that time. And there is always, in any period, a body of disciplined members. Some individuals crave submission to absolute authority. Others gradually become so dependent on the party, psychologically and intellectually and socially, that they cannot conceive of breaking with it even when its discipline irks them. When an individual has accepted three or four changes of line, reversing his stated opinions each time, he does not have much left with which he can resist. And while the party may tolerate less disciplined members for the sake of what they can do for it, it is on the disciplined members that it counts for its important tasks.

The great evil of Communism is not that it uses vicious persons, as it sometimes does, but that it corrupts good ones. In 1941, two years after leaving the party, I wrote that I had never had great respect for the party leadership and that my opinion of it had declined, but that I still had a high opinion of the rank and file. "Of the admirable persons I have known in my life," I wrote, "a considerable proportion belonged—and some still belong—to the Communist party." I should have to modify that opinion now, but the fact remains that most of the persons I knew in the party were hard-working, self-sacrificing, generous, idealistic. Most of them, fortunately, got out of the party before they were wholly corrupted, but not all.

Those of us who did get out find it hard now to explain, even to ourselves, why our eyes were not opened sooner. Again and again, between 1935 and 1939, I was troubled by events in Russia, especially the trials for treason of men who had been held up to us as heroes of the revolution. I felt that if the Old Bolsheviks were guilty, then corruption had gone deep in the Communist party of Russia; if they were innocent, the trials were outrageous. Yet it was true, I thought, that Russia was the bulwark of anti-fascism in Europe and that the Communist party was leading the fight against fascism in America, and I convinced myself that I had no right to let my private doubts interfere with this great struggle against evil.

My reasoning, viewed in retrospect, falls short of the highest standards of logic, but at least it had the advantage of putting me out on a limb that was just about to snap. In the spring of 1939 Edward Lodge Curran, a follower of Father Coughlin, challenged me to a debate in Boston. In the course of my remarks I quoted from the constitution of the Communist party:

The Communist Party of the United States upholds the democratic achievements of the American people. It opposes with all its power any clique, group, circle, faction or party which conspires or acts to subvert, undermine, weaken or overthrow any or all institutions of American democracy whereby the majority of the American people have obtained power to determine their own destiny in any degree.

"Father Curran no doubt will tell you," I said, "that this is a trick, that we don't really believe it. Be reasonable. How far would a party get if it told people one thing when it asked them to become members and something else when they had become members? Even if our leaders had some design contrary to that statement in the party constitution, they would be helpless against the members of the party."

I believed that, and I was wrong. Within six months the leaders had reversed their position on fascism, without any attempt to consult the will of the members. Moscow cracked the whip; the leaders jumped; and the rank and file did an about-face or got out. Not only because I was still above all else an anti-fascist, but even more because I saw how mistaken I had been with regard to the party, I had no choice but to quit.

IV

The Red Decade

It was chiefly among the intellectuals that Communism made its great gains in the thirties. As we have seen, most of the intellectuals were dissatisfied with our Big Business civilization when it was prospering, and the depression convinced many of them that it could and should be abolished. I have already spoken of the fifty-two writers and artists who signed the Foster-Ford manifesto in 1932. Few of these were party members, but all of them lent their support, for longer or shorter periods, to party fronts. Later, in the Popular Front period, many of the "smartest, best-educated people" joined the party, which made its influence felt in schools and colleges, publishing houses, magazine and newspaper offices, theaters, movie studios, and radio stations. In this way it was able to have an effect on the thinking of a great many people.

How great an effect? That is a question that has to be considered, for the answer one gives to it has a bearing on the problem of fighting Communism today. Some commentators talk as if the Communists had dominated the intellectual life of America in the thirties. One writer (Irving Kristol in *Commentary*) says that "the major segment of American liberalism" was following the party line. Another (John Chamberlain in *The Freeman*) declares that in the thirties the Communists captured "New York, the word capital of the United States," and thus "managed to poison the intellectual life of a whole nation." Increasingly I encounter references of this kind, until I have come to feel that a myth is taking shape—the myth of the Red Decade. W. H. Chamberlin (also in *The Freeman*) goes so far as to suggest that it was more dangerous to be an anti-Communist in the thirties and early forties than it is to be a Communist today. This is certainly a myth and, as I shall try to show later on, a myth that can do a great deal of harm.

As a Communist in the thirties I felt, and rejoiced to feel, that I belonged to a movement that was growing in influence. Yet as a writer, a publisher's adviser, and a teacher, I was never conscious of the kind of power in the intellectual world that John Chamberlain attributes to the Communists. Far from capturing "the word capital of the United States," we won only small and precarious victories. There never was a time when anti-Communism wasn't a vastly easier road to success than Communism, and if Communists engaged in persecution, as they did when they could, they were more often on the receiving end.

Let me tell of what I know, beginning with the publishing business. I suppose that in the thirties almost every publishing house in the country had at least one Communist or Communist sympathizer on its staff. In many instances the political views of these men and women were known to their colleagues and superiors; in others they were suspected; in others they were more or less successfully kept secret.

It is also true that many books sympathetic to Communism were published in these years, and frequently, I am sure, it was a Communist editor who brought in a Communist book. But that doesn't mean that these books were always, or even as a general rule, "put over" by these editors. What people forget is that there was a market for left-wing books in the thirties. You don't have to assume that there was a Communist conspiracy to explain why Knopf, Harper's, Harcourt Brace, Doubleday Doran, Random House, and most of the other respectable firms brought out some pro-Communist books; they were simply behaving like publishers. When the firm of John Day cooperated with a Communist magazine, the *New Masses*, in offering a prize for the best proletarian novel, it was a victim not of a conspiracy but of an illusion that proletarian novels would sell. Pro-Communist books would have appeared if there hadn't been a Communist editor in the whole United States.

The Macmillan Company published my book, *The Great Tradition*, in 1933, with full awareness that it purported to be a Marxist study of American literature. In 1935 the same firm not only brought out a revised edition even more explicitly Communist than the original but brought it out in cooperation with International Publishers, the official Communist publishing house. In 1936 Macmillan published my *John Reed*, a biography of a Communist by a Communist, and was happy to have it selected by the Book Union, a book club whose Communist leanings were obvious to everyone. And during all this time the president of the company was an outspoken conservative, and none of the editors, so far as I ever discovered, was a Communist or a Communist sympathizer.

I know something about the situation at Macmillan in the

thirties, for I was one of the firm's literary advisers, and scores
of manuscripts passed through my hands. Naturally my judg-
ments were influenced by the fact that I was a Communist, and
this was taken for granted by the editors. It was so definitely
taken for granted that I couldn't have put anything over. I
recommended a certain number of books that were sympathetic to Communism, but I recommended them for what
they were and on the grounds that they would sell. I also
recommended, on the same grounds, some anti-Communist
books, including Arthur Koestler's first novel, *The Gladiators.*
On the other hand, the company published at least one pro-
Communist book—Henri Barbusse's *Stalin*—that I never saw
until it was in print.

The policy that I followed in my work for Macmillan was,
I like to think, a matter of integrity, but it was also plain common sense. After all, an editor or adviser who recommends a
series of unsuccessful books, whether out of bias or out of bad
judgment, doesn't last long. For that reason Communists in
other publishing firms were obliged to adhere generally to the
same policy, whether they liked it or not. No matter how eager
they were to serve the cause, there was only so much that they
could do.

As people forgot then and forget now, it is one thing to get
a book published and another to get it read. In the late thirties
a firm called Modern Age Books was founded to publish both
reprints and new books in paper-bound editions. Modern Age
was a pioneer in this field, which has subsequently become so
important, but the company lasted only a few years, and one
reason for its failure was the fact that Communists got themselves into key positions.

Modern Age did a lot for the Communists. It employed a number of them, and it gave Communist writers some substantial advances. And it published, along with much else, of course, a lot of party-line books. Some of these, including my own *I Like America,* did fairly well, but the majority were flops. Even when the party pushed them for all it was worth, they would not move. The backers poured in money, but the firm tottered and fell, and a number of loyal Communists went looking for jobs.

The story of Modern Age is comic in many ways, but for me it has an unpleasant smell. When I think how indignant I would have been in the thirties if there had been a publishing house staffed by fascists and devoted to fascist books, I feel very unhappy about Modern Age and the part I played in its operations as one of its authors and as an editorial adviser. If there were such a house in existence today, I would denounce it as promptly and as heartily as I would have denounced a fascist concern in 1939, or would denounce one today. Yet it would be easy to exaggerate the evil that Modern Age was able to accomplish. If some of its books may have had a wide influence, most of them, I believe, were bought almost exclusively by people who were already convinced Communists. And the company was ruined, in no great length of time, by its Communist activities.

In a book called *The Red Decade,* which is the bible of all those who are hot and bothered about the thirties, Eugene Lyons has a chapter, "Intellectual Red Terror," in which he argues that pressure was used to prevent the publication of anti-Communist books and that such books, if they appeared, were attacked and vilified. I know of only one attempt to suppress a book, and Mr. Lyons mentions only one, and they happen to be the same. Party members did try to keep the Viking Press from publishing a book by Benjamin Stolberg about Communist influence in the CIO. The attempt failed. Perhaps other attempts succeeded, but the fact remains that many anti-Communist books were published in the thirties, none more successfully than Mr. Lyons' *Assignment in Utopia*. Nor was he the only writer who was able to express disillusionment with the Soviet Union; he himself speaks of Andrew Smith, Fred Beal, Jan Valtin, Freda Utley, and the Tchernavins. In fact, all the writers he mentions as victims of the intellectual red terror—John Dewey, Max Eastman, James Farrell, John Dos Passos, William Henry Chamberlin, and others—found publishers in the thirties.

Of course the Communist press attacked anti-Communist and anti-Soviet books, and in the heyday of the Popular Front there were, as Mr. Lyons says, strategically placed reviewers who, if not Communists, tended to reflect the Communist line. But it was not my impression then, and it is not my impression now, that the Communists had things their own way. In the autumn of 1934 I wrote an article for the *New Masses* in which I argued that the *New York Times Book Review* assigned almost all books on Russia to anti-Communists, usually to Russian enemies of the Soviet regime. I further pointed out that the editor and several of the principal reviewers went out of their way to sneer at and belittle American writers known to be sympathetic to Communism. Mr. Lyons can call my article part of the "intellectual red terror" if he wants to, but the fact remains that the *New Masses* was an obscure Communist publication with a circulation of a few thousand, whereas the *Times Book Review* was the most influential organ of its kind in the country.

A good deal less influential than the *Times,* but with a considerable following among the intellectuals, was the weekly magazine *The Nation.* In the later thirties the editorial policy of the *Nation* followed fairly closely the Popular Front line, but the book section was under the direction first of Joseph Wood Krutch and then of Margaret Marshall, both of whom were anti-Communists. In 1937 I wrote another article for the *New Masses* in which I pointed out that Miss Marshall was drawing a large share of her reviewers from the rapidly expanding group of men and women who, after some contact with Stalinism, had grown disillusioned. Pro-Communist books, I observed, were always given to people who could be counted on not to like them, and I made a long list. To all intents and purposes, the *Nation*'s book-review section was an organ for those anti-Communists who, according to Mr. Lyons, were having such a bad time.

We felt—make no mistake about it—that we were the victims, that we were the ones who were being persecuted. The big magazines, those that paid good money, were notoriously hostile not only to Communism and the Soviet Union but to virtually all the ideas advocated by the Popular Front. An individual writer for one of these magazines might be a Communist sympathizer, but he was both smart and lucky if he got away with any propaganda.

In fact, Communism scarcely made a dent on any of the media that reached the masses of the American people—the popular magazines, the movies, the radio. Congressional investigations have revealed that some Hollywood writers and actors were Communists or fellow travelers at one time or another, but they have not shown that these Communists influenced in any significant way the actual making of moving pictures. I remember how excited we were back in the thirties over advance reports on *Blockade,* which, we were told, was going to strike a great blow for the Loyalist cause in Spain. But when the picture was released, it did not even indicate on which side the hero was fighting. During the war a couple of pictures appeared that were favorable to the Soviet Union, but no more favorable than our official policy at that time. The Hollywood Communists have no doubt been useful to the party, to which they have given large sums of money and which they may have helped in other ways, but I am still waiting for someone to point out to me an American movie that actually contains Communist propaganda. And if there ever has been any propaganda, it has been a tiny drop in a large bucket running over with traditional American sentiments.

The same thing is true of radio. There were commentators in the thirties who seemed to accept the Popular Front slogans, but most of them were extremely cautious. As a rule, the Communists in radio who have been exposed have been actors or script writers, as unable to influence policy as their Hollywood brethren. Communists in the radio industry may have exerted a malign influence, particularly in the unions, but their propaganda achievements have been slight.

The black picture that Lyons paints has little relation to the reality that I recall. Speaking of "the intellectual and moral red terror," he says, "It could bar you from house parties on Park Avenue, jobs in Hollywood, places on the relief rolls of your city, fair treatment in the columns of great conservative papers, a hearing before supposedly broad-minded public lecture forums, access to Federal projects." Perhaps Communists did all these things at one time or another in one place or another, but this does not mean that they could do them all the time and everywhere.

If we need further proof that Lyons exaggerates the Red influence, he furnishes it for us. In the spring of 1939 a group of men and women, calling itself the Committee for Cultural Freedom, endorsed a statement that Lyons had prepared, denouncing totalitarianism as it existed in Germany, Italy, Spain, Japan, *and Russia.* "More than 140 men and women in intellectual pursuits had signed this statement by the time it was made public in May," Lyons says. "Scores of additional adhesions to this basic formulation of free men's faith came in from all over the country." And this in spite of the intellectual red terror!

There was, of course, a Communist counterattack—an open letter protesting against "attempts to bracket the Soviet Union with the Fascist states." Mr. Lyons gets a good deal of understandable amusement from the fact that this letter appeared just nine days before the Soviet-Nazi nonaggression pact, which made a lot of those of us who signed it feel silly—and worse than silly. But perhaps the important thing to notice about the pro-Soviet letter is that its signers seem rather less distinguished than the signers of the anti-Soviet statement. Comparing the two lists of names, one gets the impression that anti-Communism—and this was anti-Communism, not just non-Communism—was the dominant intellectual force. If it was not on August 14, 1939, it certainly was a fortnight later.

It is also important to observe that five of the signers of the Committee for Cultural Freedom's statement had been among the fifty-two intellectuals who endorsed the Communist candidate for President back in 1932, and at least half a dozen more had been in some sense fellow travelers. Even in the thirties, when Communism seemed so powerful, it was constantly losing adherents among the intellectuals. The party used the intellectuals for all they were worth, but its leaders were aware, as most people today are not, that there were limits beyond which most of them could not be used. To say this is no kind of defense of myself or anyone else, but the fact has to be taken into account.

The fact is particularly important when we turn to the question of Communism in education. Many teachers, especially college teachers, were Communists or sympathizers in the thirties. Like other intellectuals, they saw the great depression as proof of the collapse of capitalism, and they had some special grievances of their own. They had been badly paid even before the depression, and a lot of them had been pushed around by the businessmen who dominated the boards of trustees of the private colleges. Teachers were constantly being told about the glories of freedom of thought and speech, but in practice they discovered that discretion was essential to professional advancement. Most teachers conformed, but a certain number rebelled, and some of these became Communists.

Again it is hard to remember how much the atmosphere has changed. Today Communist teachers are charged with disloyalty to the government, conspiracy in the interests of a foreign power, and the surrender of intellectual integrity. In

the thirties, however, they were denounced for being against
the capitalist system. In the spring of 1935, as I was completing
my sixth year as assistant professor of English at Rensselaer
Polytechnic Institute, I was abruptly notified that my services
were no longer needed. Since I had been taking part in various
Communist activities for the past three years, I was not surprised by my dismissal, but I was surprised by the assertion of
Edwin C. Jarrett, the acting president, that it was purely a
matter of economy. During the next few weeks, while there
was considerable agitation regarding this breach of academic
freedom, he stuck to his story. But in speaking to the alumni
at Commencement time, Jarrett said, "We were founded by
a capitalist of the old days. We have developed and prospered
under the capitalistic regime. The men we have sent forth
and who have become industrial leaders have, in their generosity and for the benefit of the youth of the country, richly
endowed us. . . . If we are condemned as the last refuge of
conservatism, let us glory in it."

That same June, Silas H. Strawn, former president of the
American Bar Association, was the Commencement orator at
Middlebury College in Vermont. After saying, "One of the
guarantees of the Federal Constitution is the freedom of
speech," he continued, "Recently we have heard much about
'red' activities in the colleges and universities of the country.
I am unable to sympathize with the elastic conscience of those
who inveigh against the capitalistic system while on the pay-
roll of a college or university whose budget, or whose existence,
is due to the philanthropic generosity of those whose industry
and frugality have enabled them to make an endowment."

No member of the Middlebury faculty was likely to miss

the point, for earlier that spring each of them had received a letter from President Paul D. Moody, significantly headed, "Don't rock the boat." "We do not want our students to be thoughtless," President Moody informed his teachers, "nor do we want to tell them what to think. But we do not want them to go off at half-cock. Least of all do we want them to go out of class quoting us as anarchists, communists, atheists, free lovers, as, I regret to say, now and then some student does. In all that is said about capital and labor, public utilities and government, marriage and divorce, social customs, the liquor question, and a dozen and one other matters, we cannot be too guarded." He concluded, "I should feel justified in requesting, in these days as I might not in others, the resignation of any who are unwilling or unable to subordinate their private views to the interests of the College. . . . I hope that what I have said will not be regarded as in any way a desire to dictate what you shall think, or to interfere with your private views."

Middlebury teachers, in other words, were free to think as they pleased, but they had to be very careful about what they said. They were not quite so badly off as radio announcers, since words were not actually put into their mouths, but if they disagreed with the administration in any important way, they could keep it to themselves or lose their jobs. They had better forget what they had been taught in their younger days about freedom of inquiry and freedom of expression being the bases of education.

Something was wrong, but that did not justify the acceptance of Communism. Communism denies teachers freedom of any kind, and rebels are likely to be punished, not with dis-

missal but with death. However, the words of the Jarretts
and the Strawns do help to explain why some teachers were
in a mood for desperate remedies. Most of the teachers who
turned to Communism refused to admit the extent of Soviet
tyranny, but, whatever excuses they invented to salve their
consciences, they did know that academic freedom was sharply
restricted in Russia. What they told themselves was that
academic freedom was also restricted in the United States,
and that one had to choose between Communism and real or
potential fascism. The second proposition was false, but the
truth of the first gave it a certain plausibility.

The number of teachers who were Communists or fellow
travelers was never, of course, more than a tiny fraction of the
teachers in the country. The vital question, however, is how
much influence they were able to exert. The other day, speaking at a college for teachers, I was asked whether, if I were a
college president, I would permit Communists to teach. I
replied that this was a problem on which my views had changed
more than once. At the moment, I said, I was inclined to feel
that I would retain, or even hire, an avowed Communist who
was competent in his field, but that I would fire anyone who
had concealed his Communist affiliation. I put this forward
not as a solution of much practical importance but as a way
of indicating that I saw little reason to be afraid of Communism when it was in the open.

My answer shocked a young woman, who drew a startling
picture of a Communist teacher, luring his students on with
his pleasant manners, winning great popularity among them,
and seducing vast numbers to their eternal damnation. When
she had finished, I could only say, "You don't have much faith

in the other teachers." Her kind of argument, which I have heard again and again in a variety of forms, always assumes that Communist teachers are phenomenally persuasive, and non-Communist teachers phenomenally dumb.

My own situation at R.P.I. was not unlike the one that the young woman and I were talking about. My position as fellow traveler was well known, for, writer-fashion, I had recorded my conversion, step by step, in the public press, and from January 1, 1934, on, I was on the editorial staff of a Communist magazine, the *New Masses*. Because my position was known, I had to behave in my teaching job as I behaved in my Macmillan job: I leaned over backward to keep my biases out of the classroom, and I called attention to them when they forced their way in. But even if I had done my level best to convert my students, how much headway could I have made against the several hundred members of the faculty who were thoroughly committed to the capitalist system? The exponents of capitalism, moreover, felt perfectly free to express their views in the classroom—this was not at all the sort of thing Acting President Jarrett had in mind when he deplored the raising of "controversial" issues—whereas I, whatever my wishes, had to be careful about what I said.

Later, when I was for one year a counselor in American Civilization at Harvard College, I was a member of a Communist party branch made up of faculty members. It was this branch that was investigated in February 1953 by the House Committee on Un-American Activities, and testimony indicated that its maximum membership was fifteen. As I pointed out to the committee, fifteen Communists, all in the lower academic grades, is not an impressive proportion of a large faculty—1878 teachers, according to the *World Almanac* for 1939—at a time when the intellectual atmosphere was favorable to Communism and the party's Popular Front line was supposed to be especially appealing to teachers.

After I had been subpoenaed by the House Committee, I tried to recall as much as I could about the meetings of that branch. We discussed many different subjects: Marxism, the Soviet Union and the way it was maligned in the capitalist press, the dangers of fascism, the Spanish civil war, the policies of the university administration, our plans for the Teachers Union, and the manifold and exhausting activities that were part of the Popular Front movement. But I could not remember that we ever talked about how we could carry on Communist propaganda in the classroom, and on this score the testimony of the other witnesses confirmed my impression. The point is, I think, that, although we were, or believed ourselves to be, convinced Communists and were anxious to win converts, we knew there were limits. Some of us felt that there were limits beyond which we should not go; all of us felt that there were limits beyond which we could not go.

Some Communist teachers, I am sure, went as far as they could in presenting the Communist view of their subjects, but few of them were so situated that they could go very far. How much influence they had on their students is anybody's guess, but certainly they had less than is supposed by those who, like the young woman I just mentioned, have swallowed the myth of the irresistibility of the Communist arts of seduction. In the thirties a considerable number of students joined the Young Communist League or belonged to one or another of the party fronts, and some of them, I am sure, were influenced by Communist teachers, but for the most part they were responding to the same influences as the teachers were. Communism was in the air, and a certain number of people were bound to catch it.

And again we must take account of the progress of disillusionment. Of the Communist teachers I knew, the majority broke with the party a long time ago. The others, so far as I can make out, have mostly been driven out of academic life, some because they were exposed as Communists, others because their dogged fidelity to the shifting party line rendered them obviously incompetent as teachers.

The party could catch the intellectuals, but by and large it couldn't hold them. A good many of the most ardent anti-Communists today, including some of those who are responsible for the myth of the Red Decade, were themselves, at least for brief periods, under Communist influence. They recovered, and so did a larger proportion of their associates than they are willing to admit. I have already pointed out that five of the fifty-two signers of the 1932 Manifesto for Foster and Ford were outspoken anti-Communists even before the Soviet-Nazi pact. Many of the others joined the anti-Communist ranks shortly thereafter. When the Cultural and Scientific Conference for World Peace, a big party front, was held at the Waldorf-Astoria in 1949, the list of sponsors included nine of the names that had appeared on the 1932 manifesto. To me it is appalling that nine so-called intellectuals could follow the party line for seventeen years. But, statistically speaking, nine out of fifty-two isn't much of a showing.

The significance of disillusionment, moreover, is not merely statistical. The fact that so many intellectuals have been disillusioned indicates that a lot of them were not very good Communists to begin with. At the hearings I attended in Washington, as at other hearings of the sort, extracts were read from the writings of Lenin and Stalin to show what membership in the Communist party is supposed to mean. Such extracts, together with the autobiographies of Whittaker Chambers and Elizabeth Bentley, who tried hard to be good Communists, have created in the public mind a picture of the perfectly disciplined party member, ready to obey without hesitation any command his superiors may give him. That is unquestionably the party ideal, but, as I said in the preceding chapter, it is an ideal to which many Communists do not measure up, and in the later thirties the party did not even try to impose this kind of discipline on all its members. We know now that some of the intellectuals who joined the party in the thirties were willing to engage in espionage on behalf of the Soviet Union, but I believe that most of the party members I knew would have quit if they had been asked to steal documents, and I am sure that the party leaders were aware of this.

What I am saying is that the intellectuals who swallowed Communism, including myself, were to a great extent suckers. As I admitted at the outset, it is no defense whatever for an intellectual to say that he was duped, since that is what, as an intellectual, he should never allow to happen to him. We were taken in by ideas we should have seen through and people we should have suspected. And being writers and publicists, we

proceeded to take in other people, which is why the party
bothered with us in the first place. Our hands are by no means
clean, but that is no reason why we should be condemned for
crimes we didn't commit.

My purpose in criticizing the myth of the Red Decade is not
to apologize for the Communist intellectuals but to try to ar-
rive at an accurate estimate of Communist influence in the
thirties. One of the best-informed students of the subject,
Daniel Bell, has written: "Although communism *never* won
a mass following in the United States, it did have a disproportionate influence in the cultural field. At one time, from 1936
to 1939, through the fellow travelers in the publishing houses,
radio, Hollywood, the magazines, and other mass media, it
exercised influence on public opinion far beyond the number
of party members." That, I think, is absolutely true; but,
though the influence of the party was disproportionate to its
membership, it was not unlimited. As I have tried to show,
Communism did not dominate American culture in the
thirties.

I have limited myself in this chapter to cultural matters
since it is only of them that I can speak out of firsthand knowledge. Note, however, what Mr. Bell says—that Communism
never won a mass following. It is true that Communists were
active in the labor movement in the later thirties, especially
in the CIO's big drive to unionize the steel, automobile, rubber, glass, packing, and other industries, and in some unions
they entrenched themselves so well that it took years of bitter
struggle to take control away from them. (There are a few
unions in which they are still powerful.) There was only a

brief period, however, in which their influence was wide-spread, and even during this period they failed to win any large number of workers to the Communist cause.

We also know that there were Communists in many departments of the government in the thirties and early forties, and we know that some of these men and women were engaged in espionage. How many Communists there were in the government and how much influence they exerted is hard to guess, but several determined efforts to prove that the Roosevelt administration was dominated by Communists have failed. If there were New Dealers who were friendly to the Communism of the Popular Front period, there were others who were intensely suspicious of it, and they were in the majority.

What is clear, in any case, is that the party achieved whatever political power it had by means of infiltration and subterfuge. The Communist vote has never amounted to anything, and even in the worst of the depression there wasn't a chance of electing a Communist to any office of importance anywhere. Even the parties behind which the Communist party has hidden—the American Labor party in New York State, the Progressive party in the national elections of 1948 and 1952—have never acquired real strength.

But why worry about the myth of the Red Decade? Well, for one thing, it's nice to keep the record straight, but what is more important is that the myth is doing serious damage to our national morale. Every time somebody says, "Boy, the Reds nearly got us in the thirties," his listeners shiver, thinking, "It might happen again." The significant, the hopeful point, as Frederick Lewis Allen suggests in *The Big Change*, is that it never did happen. Even in the early thirties, when millions of people were hungry and desperate, the Communists polled barely 100,000 votes. Even in the later thirties, when the Popular Front had captured the allegiance of many intellectuals, the party made almost no impression on the solid anti-Communism of the great majority of the American people. Even when Communism tried to disguise itself as Twentieth-Century Americanism, the party could not count more than a hundred thousand members and a few hundred thousand sympathizers. A hundred thousand disciplined Communists might have been something to think twice about, but most sympathizers were as far from the Leninist ideal as most churchgoers are from the Christian ideal, and they soon found plenty of reason for backsliding.

Later I try to show in detail why Communism has to be taken seriously, but I think we ought to get rid of the idea, once and for all, that the Communists were ever on the verge of taking over this country. The really remarkable thing is that Communism achieved so little influence in a period that was so favorable to its growth. Recognizing that, we should be able to face confidently the threat of Communism today.

V

The End of an Era

There was chaos on the Left in the weeks after the Soviet-Nazi pact. Many persons—there is no way of knowing how many—dropped out of or were expelled from the Communist party, and the casualties were even greater among the fellow travelers than among party members. The Popular Front had been built on the foundation of anti-fascism, and that foundation had been pulverized by the pact. The *Nation* and the *New Republic,* which had been in effect organs of the Popular Front, were suddenly filled with articles criticizing Russia. Foreign correspondents, such as Louis Fischer and Vincent Sheean, who for many years had been favorably interpreting the policies of the Soviet Union, not only denounced the pact but expressed doubts, hitherto concealed, about the whole Stalinist regime. As Fischer was subsequently to confess in his autobiography, he had watched with increasing dismay the growth of Stalinist terrorism, but he had kept his misgivings to himself because of his belief that the Soviet Union was in any case a bulwark against fascism. When that illusion collapsed, it brought down all his other illusions.

For many persons the autumn of 1939 was a period of anguished reconsideration of all they had believed. As soon as reports of my resignation were published, I began to hear

from some of these persons, and after my statement of the
reasons for my resignation appeared in the *New Republic,* the
letters poured in. Some were congratulatory, some critical,
some merely questioning. A novelist, who said that my book,
I Like America, had made him a fellow traveler in the first
place, described the effect of the pact on him and his wife.
"What had been the stuff of the proudest battle of mankind
had turned into grisly, demeaning burlesque. That, anyway,
was how we—too emotionally, maybe—felt. But we found
ourselves wondering how *you* would feel and react, whether
you'd give us any example we could honor, imitate. You did,
and we thank you for it a second time. So, I imagine, must
many others. Your recent actions and statements must have
cost you much deep feeling and peculiar courage, a sacrifice
of many years' stiffening standpoint—and they practically demand this truly grateful realization of that cost to you."

On the other hand, there were letters from the people who
had decided to stay with the party. Not a few of these were
friendly and rather touching: "It is with sadness and indeed a sense of loss that I hear of your resignation," or, "I may
be saying what is fairly obvious when I say that I was deeply
hurt when I learned of your decision to resign from the Communist party." A young woman wrote: "Granville, if someone had told me I was to inherit a million, I wouldn't have
been more stunned than when I read of your sudden departure." And a young man: "Your action this week has un-
doubtedly dealt an awful blow, whether you intended that or
not."

Some of the Communists sought to win me back: "Comrade, why do you now desert the only force which speaks al-

ways and consistently for the American workers, the only party truly and unselfishly dedicated to fight for them through every difficulty? I ask you to reconsider your action and to declare publicly your devotion to the cause of justice and humanity by rejoining the ranks of the front-line fighters for this cause." Some were more emphatic: "You have let a lot of us down, and I sincerely regret it," or, "We look forward to seeing and hearing from you again when you come to your senses.' A correspondent filled two sides of a sheet of paper with, "Now is the time for all good men to come to the aid of their Party." Two or three persons intimated that I either was moved by fear or had been bought off.

Many of my friends, naturally, were either party members or close fellow travelers, and we wrote one another long letters full of unhappy speculations. To most of the fellow travelers it was clear from the very beginning that they could no longer accept the leadership of the party. I remember that one of them said to me, the day after the pact was announced, "For four years I've envied you; now I'm sorry for you." Another wrote: "My attitude toward the CP is one of distrust. The party bet its pants, shirt, and g-string on Russia (and those of everyone else who accepted its analyses and followed its line) and lost to the last stitch. It clings more desperately than ever to the Russian connection as the be-all and end-all of its existence, and insists that people continue to 'trust' Russia (i.e., to take on faith what it says about Russia) and accept lines built on what it thinks is Russia's orientation. Those who peddle a gold brick twice over ought not to be surprised if they get the door slammed in their faces."

Party members, as a rule, found it harder to make up their

minds. One friend, who had agreed with me that we should get out of the party and try to start an independent, non-Communist, left-wing organization, suddenly wrote: "I have decided, thinking over the history of the radical movement in this country and elsewhere, that we will condemn ourselves to impotence as far as any progressive movement is concerned if we go ahead with the plans we originally discussed, and that we will probably do irremediable harm. I think the choice is either to stick with the party or to retire completely from politics for the time being. I shall do the first." A few weeks later he reversed himself again and broke with the party.

Readers of Chambers, Budenz, and Elizabeth Bentley are likely to think of a break with the party as highly dramatic. In terms of the psychology of the person involved, the action is dramatic enough, but in the majority of cases there is no outward drama. This was particularly true in the months after the Soviet-Nazi pact. The party was in a state of confusion, and it took cognizance of that fact by setting up a period for "free" discussion. The discussion was free only in the sense that a man could say what he thought without being immediately denounced as a Trotskyite or a fascist. If, however, he did not eventually accept the new party line, that was the end of him. During this period many persons simply stopped going to party meetings. Others were expelled. One of my friends felt that the only way to give the party a fair test was to stay in and see what happened. "The ax fell last night in a regular Moscow trial," he wrote me with obvious relief. "No previous warning, ridiculous charges, and the meeting postponed from last week until they were sure of a majority."

The great problem for the people who were breaking with the party was what they ought to do next and what they could do. One of the strongest appeals of the party was the fact that it kept you busy. If you belonged to the party, you were proud of being a doer rather than a talker, and even if what you did seemed pretty trivial, the Marxist dialectic assured you that your work had ultimate historical significance. When you left the party because you believed that what it was doing was wrong, you felt that you must immediately discover what was right. The sheer habit of continual activity made you miserable in idleness.

Many of the comrades who wrote to protest my decision felt that I had stepped off into a void of impotence and loneliness. "The important thing now, Comrade, is what can you do? Nothing! You have tied yourself hand and foot, and, what is more, you have gagged yourself." Or, "Have you really considered? Do you know what it will do to you to do this, after you have gone through so much for the party and Communism has been the central core of your life?" As a man who had just quit wrote me, "Many good comrades look with disgust at the *Daily Worker* nowadays, yet remain with the CP *faute de mieux*."

The friend who decided to stick with the party had said that the only alternative was "to retire from politics for the time being." Some ex-Communists made that choice. One of them wrote: "The past few months, in my case, have been spent in contemplation rather than action. As a result I have joined no other organizations. I have been looking, not for an ideology, but for a humanitarian philosophy of life according to which I could chart my activities as an individual.

I want to help mankind, not to save mankind, and, in helping, I do not wish to enforce my conception of what is good or what is right on my neighbor. Perhaps the best thing the intellectual can do, after all, is to secure a good grandstand seat on Mount Olympus and let nothing dislodge him from it, no matter how uncomfortable things get down below or how strong the urge becomes to rush into the mundane fray."

To most of us at that point, however, the climate of Olympus had no appeal. We wanted action. Why not, we were saying to ourselves, take the Popular Front away from the Communists—or, more accurately, since they had smashed it, why not put it together again without the Communist connections? After all, we were still anti-fascists, and we still believed in socialism as a goal. All that had been wrong with the Popular Front of the 1935–39 period, we argued, was the fact that it had been tied to the Communist party and hence to the exigencies of Soviet foreign policy. An independent, an American Popular Front, we told ourselves, could be a great force for progress.

In the autumn and winter of 1939–40 I attended a number of conferences on the question of forming an organization, tentatively called the Independent Left, and I also issued a little mimeographed bulletin in which anyone who wanted to could express his ideas about what ought to be done. Immediately it became apparent that American radicalism had been split a dozen different ways. Although all my correspondents were out of sympathy with the Communist party, some continued to defend the policies of the Soviet Union, while others, like myself, were increasingly convinced that there was little to choose between Russian Communism and German Nazism. Some considered themselves simon-pure Marxists, and attacked Stalinism from a Marxist point of view, but others, again like myself, were beginning to question the whole structure of Marxism. Some supported the New Deal, but many urged a bolder advance in the direction of socialism. To some World War II, then in its dormant phase, was an anti-fascist war, whereas others argued that it was a clash between rival imperialisms.

After the conquest of France in the spring of 1940, the war issue was the one that counted most, and the non-Communist Left was soon irreconcilably split between the interventionists and the anti-interventionists, with the former supporting Roosevelt and the latter backing Norman Thomas. By this time most of the ex-Communists and ex-fellow travelers had found individual answers, more or less satisfying, to the question of what to do.

For my own part, I had become increasingly distrustful of ambitious, all-inclusive schemes for the making over of society. I could agree with one of my correspondents, a sociologist, who wrote: "I think that the modest aims of the New Deal, or the CIO, or the ILGWU have a more direct and effective result in reshaping our society than the all-encompassing aspirations of the CP or, for that matter, of the Socialist party. I believe that such has been the case with most significant changes: the movements that operate within the existing framework and prepare public sentiment for piece-meal and apparently hopelessly inadequate changes are the ones that bring progress." I also began to have more sympathy with the correspondent who wanted to move to Mount Olympus. Even if one didn't choose to stay there, I said to myself, it might be salutary to take a look at the view. More practically, since I knew that I was an activist by temperament, I decided to be active where I could test what I was doing by observable results—specifically in the small town in which I lived.

But to return to the situation in the fall of 1939. One thing was clear: the prestige Communism had briefly enjoyed among the intellectuals was dead. Declining even before the pact, it had been struck a mortal blow on the day Von Ribbentrop flew to Moscow. Some intellectuals, it is true, stuck with the party all through the period in which it was denouncing the war as an imperialist war and was doing its best to prevent the United States from giving effective aid to beleaguered Britain. And after Germany invaded Russia on June 22, 1941, and the party began clamoring for American participation, a few intellectuals came creeping back. But even during the Soviet-American alliance, when all Communists pretended to be super-patriots and the party was almost respectable, there was no real revival of Communist prestige among the intellectuals. And Russia's postwar policy brought the party's membership and influence almost—but not quite—to the point of insignificance.

What of those who remained in the party after the pact? The letters I have already quoted suggest how much they feared the loneliness outside the party and how little they were prepared to do without the party's guidance. They had to believe that Russia was right. Because I had done so much speaking around Boston and been given so much publicity, Phil Frankfeld, the party organizer in Boston, found it advisable, when I left the party, to write me an open letter, which was widely circulated in Massachusetts. Among other things, he said, "To me it always appeared that you had an inner lack of conviction that the Soviet Union really symbolizes Socialism Victorious." And Anna Louise Strong, a foreign correspondent who was full of enthusiasm for Russia, wrote me, "Don't you know in your soul that Stalin and Molotov are our comrades?" (Some years later Stalin and Molotov informed Miss Strong that she was no comrade of theirs, and she was expelled from the Soviet Union. Mr. Frankfeld, while he was awaiting trial under the Smith Act, was accused by the party of deviations from its line and kicked out.)

The religious phraseology used by these two dialectical materialists is interesting. Both letters, remember, were written soon after the pact, before there was an official explanation of it. Confronted by such a situation, both Frankfeld and Miss Strong fell back on faith and expected me to do the same. Officially there is no room for faith in the Marxist scheme, but it is an indispensable part of the Communist make-up.

Faith verging on blind fanaticism filled another letter that I received at the same time, this one from a young woman I had never met. "So it all comes to this," she wrote, "that your whole life previous to this time, all you underwent for the party, all the privations you seem willingly to have suffered when you could have had any post you wanted anywhere in the country, all this has gone up in a puff of smoke and lost its meaning. What for? You might just as well have taken it nice and easy and saved yourself the trouble. It might just as well never have happened. What a pity to find one's life suddenly without meaning. What is left for you now? You have maintained your precious integrity. I suppose you can sit and contemplate it like some unbelievable Buddha. But unless you have guts enough to admit a mistake, you have taken the first step downward on a path which leads to a swamp. . . ."

She went on to speak of the Moscow trials. "On the morning of March 12, 1938, one A. P. Rosengoltz made the following statement: 'Woe and misfortune will betide him who strays even to the smallest extent from the general line of the Bolshevik party. I want you to believe me.' You can believe him, because a few mornings later he was shot for high treason in the Soviet Union. I guess you haven't read the account of these trials. If you start on page 714 of the last one and read just the final pleas of these men, you might still be able to draw a lesson from it before it is too late."

What I did draw a lesson from was this letter and others like it. More than anything else, the fanaticism of some of my correspondents helped me to understand what I had escaped from. Some years had been wasted, and worse than wasted, but I believed that whether my life had lost its meaning depended on me. It could, I believed, have a fairer meaning because I had had guts enough to admit a mistake.

I realized then, as I have increasingly realized since, what a force for evil Communism can be, and I was happy that I had broken with it. Yet at the same time I knew that it would be wretchedly dishonest to say that everything I had stood for and everything I had done as a Communist was evil, and what was true of me was true, often in much greater degree, of others. I resolved then and there to try to keep both of these facts in mind.

VI

What We Fight

I remember very well the moment at which we got the news of the Soviet-Nazi nonaggression pact. For some reason we had not listened to the late news the night before, and so I had been given a good night's sleep that I wasn't, so to speak, entitled to. Then at breakfast, on a beautiful summer morning, we heard the report. When I was able to speak, I said, "That knocks the bottom out of everything."

My comment, as it turned out, was singularly accurate. From the first I had a feeling that the consequences of the pact, so far as I was concerned, could only be the total rejection of Communism, and in the arguments that went on and on during the next two weeks—for we had a houseful of guests and people kept stopping in to see how we were taking it—I spoke bitterly against the Soviet Union. But in time I cooled down, and when I quit the party, it was on the grounds that the party had acted contrary to all its professed principles and had revealed its complete subservience to Russia. With regard to the Soviet Union, I said, I would wait and see.

For a case of sorts could be made for Russia. From 1935 to 1938 Russia had been the great advocate of collective security, constantly urging the Western democracies to take a firm stand against German aggression. Then in September 1938

Prime Minister Chamberlain of Great Britain had appeased Hitler at the expense of Czechoslovakia, with what seemed to be the clear intention of turning Germany against the Soviet Union. To all American anti-fascists, including countless non-Communists, this had seemed one of the worst betrayals of mankind in the whole of history. To Stalin it had showed plainly that he could not depend on England and France and that he must take care of Hitler in his own way, which he proceeded to do.

That was the case, and it had to be considered, but there were also some questions that had to be asked. If Chamberlain's Munich was a betrayal, wasn't Stalin's Munich-in-reverse equally a betrayal? It was said, of course, that Stalin had no choice: Munich had demonstrated that he must betray or be betrayed. But could not the same thing be said in defense of Chamberlain? Might he not have been convinced that if he had got himself embroiled with Hitler over Czechoslovakia, Stalin would have left England and France holding the bag? And didn't the events of 1939 suggest that Chamberlain's fears were justified, for hadn't Stalin made a deal with Hitler as soon as France and England were firmly committed to the defense of Poland?

In the weeks after the pact and the beginning of World War II the Machiavellians, both in the party and out of it, had a field day. Russia's actions, they asserted, had to be judged in terms of *Realpolitik;* moral principles were strictly irrelevant. But it was on moral grounds that I and many others had been defending the Soviet Union. Whatever Russia's shortcomings, both those we admitted publicly and those we worried about in private, we had believed that the Soviet government was working for peace, was opposed to fascism on principle, and, as Stalin had repeatedly said, did not desire a foot of alien soil. Now that government had deliberately precipitated a world war, had declared that fascism was a matter of taste, and had grabbed just as much territory as it could lay hands on.

If Russia's policies were determined by considerations of *Realpolitik,* then we had been talking nonsense from 1935 to 1939—which of course was the case. We had never doubted that Russia had a practical interest in the Popular Front, but we had believed that its purpose was to offset the growing power of fascism—that its aims and ours, in other words, were identical. But if, as its apologists now insisted, Russia had been playing the Machiavellian game all along, the purpose of the Popular Front policy had been to maneuver the democracies into a position that would permit Russia to make a deal with Hitler. It had been a sham, a dodge, a fake from start to finish.

Certainly the actions of the Communist party in America supported that conclusion. The comrades, who had been begging France and England to stand up to Hitler, now decided that these nations were fighting an imperialist war. The party defended the absorption of the Baltic republics, the partition of Poland, and the war against Finland as Soviet contributions to the cause of peace. When, after the fall of France in the spring of 1940, the United States was divided in the struggle between isolationists and interventionists, the Communists fought shoulder to shoulder with the America Firsters, contributing their own slogan, "The Yanks are not coming."

When Hitler invaded Russia in June 1941, the war was

immediately transformed into an anti-fascist crusade, and the Communists became fanatical interventionists. Like almost everyone else, I was delighted that Russia was fighting on our side rather than Hitler's, and I welcomed every Russian victory. But when American leaders talked optimistically about cooperating with Russia after the war, I kept my fingers crossed.

I did believe, however, that Russia would be so exhausted by the war that it couldn't cause much trouble, and there I was wrong. Rallying with astonishing speed, the Soviet Union established puppet governments in those adjoining countries that had been invaded by its armies, and these so-called satellite states became to all intents and purposes Russian provinces. In an article I wrote in 1946, "The Spectre That Haunts the World," I called the roll of Soviet captives: Poland, Yugoslavia, Bulgaria, Rumania, East Germany, Hungary, and Albania. Czechoslovakia, Finland, and Greece, I warned, were likely to be next on the list. I was right about Czechoslovakia and would have been right about Greece if the United States government hadn't stepped in.

For by this time—1947—the cold war had begun. Aid to Greece was an announcement that the United States would resist further aggression. The second warning—and the second victory—came with the American and British airlift, which saved Berlin for the Allies. But the great test was to come in 1950. The Communists by that time had conquered China and were on the march in half a dozen other Asiatic countries. In North Korea a puppet government had been set up after the war under the protection of Russian occupation troops. On June 10, 1950, *Izvestia*, the official newspaper of the Soviet government in Moscow, published a dispatch from Pyongyang, the North Korean capital, stating that the central committee of the Communist-dominated North Korean Patriotic Front had called for the unification of Korea, to be achieved by August 15, fifth anniversary of the liberation of that country from Japan. That was the tip-off. Two weeks later North Korean troops began the invasion of South Korea that was intended to bring about the unification. Since high American military authorities had held that South Korea was indefensible, the Communist plan seemed certain of success, but it was balked by the resolute action of the government of the United States.

Obviously the United States and the Soviet Union have been to all intents and purposes at war, and there can be no doubt that the American Communists are on Russia's side. Maintaining that South Korea invaded North Korea, they have denounced our action as an imperialist adventure and have demanded the withdrawal of American troops. They have echoed Communist charges of germ warfare and repeated every other item of Communist propaganda. They have done their best to build up sentiment against all our preparations for resistance to Communist aggression. Just as they were anti-fascists from 1935 to 1939, isolationists from 1939 to 1941, and patriots from 1941 to 1945, so now they have become great lovers of peace—a one-way peace, of course.

At each new turn the Communist party has lost a certain number of its members and supporters, but there are always the faithful. How do people get that way? I can make some guesses out of my own experience. I have admitted that, to begin with, I was dazzled—by the way Marxism explained all

mysteries and by the feeling that I not only understood but
was making history. Later I began to have doubts, but, like a
lot of other people, I suppressed them on practical grounds:
the party was doing more good than harm; Russia was at least
the great enemy of fascism; so much of Marxism was true that
there was no sense in arguing about the fine points. As I have
already acknowledged, I might have carried this even further
if I had not been so publicly committed to the anti-fascist
position of the Popular Front. I might have said to myself,
when the pact came along, "I'll wait and see," and, having
failed to protest at once against the new line, I should have
found it increasingly difficult to break with the party. If
things had worked out that way, I might have had some bad
moments between August 23, 1939, and June 22, 1941, but
then, after Russia had been invaded and the line had changed,
my suffering would have ended. I could have told myself that
the pact, the partition, the war against Finland—everything
—was justified by the fight Russia was making against the
Nazis. Russia, I could have said, had been right all the time.

I know that this sort of thing happened. We have already
seen how various Communists reacted to the pact and to my
resignation from the party. After the line had been clarified,
I was a bourgeois renegade, a Trotskyite wrecker, and an imperialist warmonger, in the eyes of all staunch and disciplined
party members. However, a few of my acquaintances, who
had decided to wait and see, remained on friendly terms with
me, and they admitted to me doubts that they concealed from
their fellow Communists. Then the invasion of Russia began,
and they hastened to tell me that the party had been right and
I had been wrong all the time. One such person wrote me in

the summer of 1941: "How can you still speak of Russia's 'appeasing' Germany? Isn't it clear that this is just what Stalin planned and that this is the only way in which the defeat of fascism could have been guaranteed? Isn't it also clear that Moscow would by now have been lost if it had not been for the protection of Poland, the Baltic States, and Bessarabia? As for Finland, I hope you see now that the Finnish government is, and always was, fascist."

Not everyone was affected in just this way by the new turn. One friend of mine, who had accepted the pact with some difficulty but had accepted it and had come out with his own conception of Russian strategy, was convinced by the Nazi thrust into the Balkans in the spring of 1941 that Russia was about to be invaded. He was at that time a member of the party fraction in a front organization opposed to American intervention, and he tried to tell his comrades that they should be preparing the way for a change of line that seemed to him inevitable. His ideas, however, were denounced by party officials, and he was about to be brought up on charges and expelled from the party when Germany crossed the Russian border and all was immediately forgiven. In that moment he saw through the great fraud, and he quit then and there.

Another friend quietly stopped going to party meetings in the fall of 1939. He just ceased to be a Communist, without becoming an anti-Communist. Some three years later, when he was an officer in the United States Army, he happened to read in the *New Masses*, to which he had once been a contributor, an article seeking to prove by statistics that the United States and Britain could invade France and establish a Second Front at that moment. He was in a position to know that the statistics were false, and suddenly it dawned on him that his erstwhile comrades were not merely lying in the interests of the Soviet Union; they would gladly sacrifice his life and the lives of thousands of American soldiers in order to help the Russian cause. He has been a militant anti-Communist ever since.

The Communist who survived those two abrupt reversals of policy in August 1939 and June 1941 was not likely to be affected by subsequent changes of line. Let us imagine such a Communist in the early years of the war, always clamoring for the Second Front, of course, but at the same time genuinely supporting the American war effort and doing so happily. In 1944 Earl Browder dissolved the Communist Party of the United States and established the Communist Political Association. "American Communists," Browder wrote, "are relinquishing for an extended period the struggle for partisan advancement for themselves as a party. The Communists foresee that the practical political aims they hold will for a long time be in agreement in all essential points with the aims of a much larger body of non-Communists and that therefore our political actions will be merged in such larger movements." Our loyal Communist applauded, and went to work to persuade unions to keep the no-strike pledge, Negroes to forget their demands for equality, and the American people in general to sacrifice everything for the sake of winning the war. And then, just a year later, when Browder was denounced by Moscow for his "deviations" and was expelled from the party, which had been reconstituted, our loyal Communist discovered that he had always had grave doubts about Browder's intelligence and integrity.

During the past eight years the going has been hard for American Communists, and many have fallen by the wayside, but a small band of the faithful has survived. Their defense of the Soviet Union has been a miracle of consistency. To them the satellites are not satellites; they are independent people's republics. Before June 28, 1948, they believed that Tito was a Communist of the highest stature; after that date they had no doubt that he was, and always had been, a tool of capitalism. Every Russian maneuver is a magnificent contribution to the cause of peace, and they never weary of denouncing the vicious American warmongers.

No one can suppose that the American Communists actually believe any large part of what they are saying at any given moment, but it is a mistake to assume that they don't believe anything. Communists, as we have seen, live by faith. This may begin as faith in Marxism, but the member of the party soon notices that official interpretations of Marx, Engels, and Lenin vary as the Moscow line varies. It may begin as faith in a particular cause—the revolution, anti-fascism, peace, war, peace again—but causes are picked up and dropped again every few years. The convert may be revolted by the injustices and inequalities he sees about him; he comes to learn that injustices and inequalities in the Soviet Union are to be regarded in an entirely different light. Anti-Semitism, for instance, a dreadful thing in Germany or the United States, was, at least for a couple of months in early 1953, a virtue in Russia and the satellite states. The convert, if he remains loyal, discovers that there can be only one abiding place for

his faith—the leadership of the Soviet Union. For many years
that faith was pinned to a man, Stalin, and it remains to be
seen whether it can be transferred to another individual. But
the faith itself seems likely to endure.

This faith can be given a semi-rational formulation. Marx
and Engels, the formula begins, presented the only true interpretation of history. This interpretation, as we have seen,
teaches that all history is the history of class struggles and that
it is only through the triumph of the proletariat that a just
and classless society can be brought about. Understanding
this, Lenin showed how the proletariat should prepare for its
task and carry it through. The revolution—*the* revolution—
triumphed in Russia in 1917. But historical conditions were
such that world revolution could not take place at that time,
and the Union of Socialist Soviet Republics was surrounded
by enemies. It thereupon became the duty of every true socialist (i.e., Communist) everywhere in the world to defend
the bastion of socialism. The strategy of this defense had to
be worked out by the commanding generals of that bastion,
who after all had shown how to win a revolution, and their
orders had to be obeyed by Communists everywhere. One
must understand that the Soviet Union, so long as it is a for-
tress, cannot develop a perfect socialist society; many things
must be endured for the sake of the future. One must also
understand that the defense of the bastion is an enterprise
fraught with both difficulty and danger, and that anyone who
would weaken that defense must be ruthlessly eliminated.
After Lenin's death there was only one man, Joseph Stalin,
who fully understood what was necessary to strengthen the
Soviet Union and thus advance the cause of World Com-

munism, and it was therefore right and proper that he was given absolute power. Though there may be difficulties for a time, the foundations he built are so strong that his work will be carried on in his spirit.

Do you remember what the organizer in Boston wrote me after I got out of the party? "To me it always appeared that you had an inner lack of conviction that the Soviet Union really symbolizes Socialism Victorious." That is exactly the kind of faith that is needed, and it must be strong enough to accept any kind and any amount of evil for the sake of the distant victory.

For most converts, Communism satisfies deep needs: it gives them a cause, a program of action, a reason for living. ("What a pity," the young woman wrote me in the fall of 1939, "to find your life suddenly without meaning.") After a time the Communist may have no friends except in or near the party, and leaving the party can mean a terrible loneliness. In spite of this, most people break away—there are several times as many ex-Communists in this country as there are Communists—but those who remain are strengthened in their faith. If a person cannot bring himself to leave the party because life outside it seems unbearable, then his faith grows big enough to justify his staying in.

I have been talking about the rank-and-file members of the party, but the same process operates, and with greater force, for party functionaries and underground workers. Their whole lives are bound up in the party, and after a time they cannot even imagine what existence outside would be like. The more deeply they are involved, the more difficult and dangerous it is for them to quit, and they therefore cling tenaciously to their faith, as the only possible justification of what in any case they have to do.

This is not to say that there are no cynics in the party. In this country at any rate it is hard to imagine anyone's joining the party for opportunistic reasons; the opportunities aren't there. But I have always suspected that there are party functionaries who, having got themselves inextricably involved, have cold-bloodedly decided to make the best of a bad situation. And there are functionaries in the party, as there are in the churches, whose faith has faded away without their realizing what has happened.

In any case cynicism and faith turn out to be shockingly similar. There are people who maintain that the Russian Bolsheviks never wanted anything but power for themselves. I doubt that, but it would make precious little difference if it were true. Having spent all their lives in winning and holding power by whatever means served the purpose, they have inevitably made power their only end. Perhaps Socialism Victorious is something they think about now and then, and perhaps it isn't; perhaps Malenkov makes jokes about it to himself while he is shaving. It doesn't matter. Like Stalin before him, Malenkov will do anything that a power-obsessed dictator will do, and nothing that such a man wouldn't do. And so it is with the functionaries in this country: nobody will ever be able to tell from their behavior which are the cynics and which have faith.

If the Communist faith is set forth in a series of propositions, there is one important conclusion that has to be drawn: world revolution is something that moves out from Russia. Soon after I had left the party, a man who had done a lot of good

work in the anti-fascist front came to see me. He said something like this: "I'm quitting, too, but not for the same reasons.
We were suckers, but it was our own fault. We ought to have
known that the Popular Front was just a trick. I see that the
party was right in using me, but it used me up, and I'm
through. There isn't anything I can do for the party any
more, but I'm not going to do anything against it." Then he
added, "I know now how the revolution is coming to the
United States: the Red Army is going to bring it when it
marches down from Alaska."

At the time I thought that last statement was intended as a
joke, but I afterward realized that there was a great truth in
it. In the course of the years since the Russian Revolution the
Marxist idea of world revolution as an international process
had been lost, and world revolution had become indistinguishable from Russian imperialism. Lenin is supposed to have
said that after the revolution had succeeded in a technically
advanced country such as Germany, Russia would have to
take a back seat. Lenin, of course, was a cosmopolitan, whereas
Stalin never knew anything at first hand about Western
Europe, but I think that Lenin, if he had lived, would have
been forced by the logic of power along the path of nationalist
communism. Would any Russian Communist leader, for
example, have dared to take a different course from Stalin's
with regard to Germany in 1932? The Communists were
strong in Germany, and there was at least a possibility that
they might have captured the country if they had launched a
revolution before Hitler seized power. From their own point
of view they had nothing to lose, since Hitler was bound to
crush the party. But if their revolution had failed, Russia

would have suffered. Since it was the first duty of the Russian leaders to preserve the revolution that had been won, they ordered the German Communists not to revolt.

We have seen how the revolution was spread in 1939—by a process of absorption. We have seen how it was spread after the war—in countries along the Russian borders, with Russian leadership. The Russian Communists would never encourage —probably would never permit—a revolution in a country that did not have common borders with the Soviet Union or with territory it controlled. Let us suppose, for example, that the Communist party had become very strong in the United States during the great depression and had actually been able to take power. Is it conceivable that the Communist rulers of America would have continued indefinitely to take orders from the Communist rulers of Russia? Certainly not. Knowing this, Stalin would have gone a long way to prevent a seizure of power if it had been imminent.

The greatest setback Russian imperialism has suffered was in Yugoslavia. Because of the strength of the military forces that had been built up in the struggle against Germany, because Yugoslavia had been liberated by the Yugoslavs and not by the Red Army, Tito was able to defy Russia. He got away with it, but the Russians have made sure, by a series of purges in the satellites, that there will never be another Tito. China, of course, because of its tremendous size and potential strength, is in a different position from the European satellites, and a conflict of interests between China and Russia is bound to happen sooner or later. Whether it will happen in time to help the democracies is another question.

Just as the establishment of Communism in one country

leads to totalitarianism and the dictatorship of a few power-greedy men, so Communist world revolution becomes indistinguishable from other brands of imperialist aggression. Communist Russia has grabbed what territory it could, and is eager to grab more. When it cannot immediately annex a country, it makes it a colony. In administering its colonies, it uses native Communists, but it does not trust them. They are supplemented with Russian-born agents, and periodically they are purged.

What world revolution means to the Russian leaders, and to good Communists everywhere, is a world-wide Union of Socialist Soviet Republics with Moscow as its capital. It is not merely, or primarily, Marxist theory that leads them to think in terms of eventual world domination. They are following the logic of all totalitarian dictators: their power is not safe until it is universal. On the other hand, they must recognize that it will take a long time to establish world-wide control. If, then, their hostility is chiefly directed against the United States, that is not because this country is down on their schedule for immediate annexation but because it stands in the way of the plans they have for Asia and Europe.

If we understand this situation, we can easily understand the character and function of the Communist party in the United States. I used to wonder, in the days after I left the party, why the Russian leaders did not give the American party at least the appearance of independence, so that it would have a chance to grow, and I thought they were stupid. I have since realized that they knew what they were doing. They were not interested in size but in subservience. They were not trying to develop a party capable of bringing about a revolution in America; they wanted a party that would serve Russian interests, a party of Soviet propagandists and Soviet agents.

Since I saw no evidence of espionage when I was a party member, I was for some time skeptical on the subject of Communist spies. A document that did a lot to enlighten me was the report of the Royal Commission on the Gouzenko case in Canada. Igor Gouzenko was sent to Canada in June 1943 as a cipher clerk on the staff of Colonel Zabotin, the Military Attaché at the Soviet Embassy in Ottawa. In August 1945 he was ordered to return to Russia with his wife and child. Disillusioned with the Soviet Union and fearful of what might happen to him there, he seized a variety of documents that would substantiate his story, and fled. After some mishaps he found protection with the police, and his papers were made the subject of a careful investigation.

Gouzenko's testimony and his documents indicated that there were at least three spy systems operating in Canada, each of them independent of the others and directly responsible to Moscow. Colonel Zabotin, as the head of one of these apparatuses, had detailed dossiers on many of his agents, most of whom were members of the Communist party of Canada. Through their activity Moscow had been supplied with a vast amount of secret information regarding Canada's military preparations. Among the agents exposed in this investigation was Dr. Alan Nunn May, the first atomic spy to be caught.

Since that time we have had plenty of evidence that similar apparatuses have been functioning in this country. Whittaker Chambers, Hede Massing, Elizabeth Bentley, and others have shown that Communists, and sometimes Communist sympathizers, in government departments have systematically turned over information to Russian agents. The trial of Julius and Ethel Rosenberg proved that here as in Canada party members are used as spies—in this instance as spies of the most dangerous sort. It becomes impossible to doubt that the Communist party is in fact closely integrated with the whole vast machine for Russian espionage in America, and that is exactly what we would expect in the light of our analysis of Russian aims and Communist practices.

Not all party members, of course, are spies, and perhaps there are some, even at this late date, who refuse to believe in the reality of Soviet espionage. But if the guilt of a particular individual cannot be taken for granted, the guilt of the party can be. The Communist party is in essence a party of Russian agents.

What we fight is the aggressiveness of Russian Communism, and we fight the Communist party in the United States because, and to the extent that, it serves that aggressiveness. The party is numerically weak at the present moment, and its influence was never smaller. Regarded simply as an American political party, or even, if you will, as an American conspiracy to overthrow the government, it could be dismissed as nothing worse than a nuisance. But there is nothing American about it; it is an agency of a hostile power, and therefore dangerous.

VII

What We Defend

Most Americans agree on the necessity of fighting Communism; the big arguments concern the methods to be used. I shall make what contribution I can to that debate, but first we might think about what we are fighting for. I said at the outset that I had found more and more reasons for liking America, and now I want to state what those reasons are.

Back in the early thirties, when I was so badly shaken by the depression, there were many directions in which I might have turned. I might have agreed with those who said that there was absolutely nothing to do about the depression except to wait for the operation of economic laws to restore prosperity. I might have joined the Technocrats, who were convinced that the engineers, if they were given a free hand, could not merely bring back prosperity but achieve utopia. I might have gone along with Francis Townsend and his scheme for old-age revolving pensions. I might have supported Huey Long and his campaign for "Share-Our-Wealth" and after his death followed the lead of his lieutenant and disciple, Gerald L. K. Smith. I might have become a member of Father Coughlin's National Union for Social Justice and, later, his Christian Front. I might have been converted by Father Divine, and gone to live in one of his "Heavens." Or I could have become, like Lawrence Dennis, an avowed Fascist.

Almost any of these courses of action would have proved more innocuous in the long run than joining the Communist party, but I cannot say that, in retrospect, I find any of them attractive. What I do wish is that I had had sense enough to see the possibilities of the New Deal.

The trouble was that by 1932, when Franklin D. Roosevelt was nominated for the Presidency, I, like John Chamberlain, had said "farewell to reform." I was suffering just then from an acute attack of what Edmund Wilson has called Marxist snow blindness, and it was as clear to me as if it had come in a revelation from on high that the capitalist system was beyond saving. "Culture and the Crisis," the pamphlet of the fifty-two for Foster and Ford, said: "Franklin D. Roosevelt purveys a mixtum compositum of Populist leavings, 'cheap money' quackery, municipal-ownership platitudes, pious welfarism, and stale dregs of economic liberalism." Obviously this would never do. "Only Socialism can eliminate the exploitation and misery which prevail under capitalism."

I believed it, and I voted for Foster and Ford. Visiting Iowa in the summer of 1933, as a representative of a Communist front, the National Committee for the Defense of Political Prisoners, I found that the farmers there, many of whom had been engaged in militant demonstrations against mortgage foreclosures, were eying the New Deal with a mixture of interest and skepticism. They were going to find out, I was certain, that skepticism was justified. It might be that their situation would be improved for a time by the New Deal, but in the end they would be worse off than before. When the

New Masses first appeared as a weekly in January 1934, with me as literary editor, it carried on its cover a cartoon by William Gropper showing FDR as a medicine man, selling bottles labeled NRA, AAA, CCC, etc. And I approved.

My great mistake, as it seems to me now, was my failure to take into account the American spirit and tradition of reform and the American gift for improvisation. Opposed to Marxist dogma, persuasive as that seemed, was a long record of American experience, and it was that record I chose to ignore. The United States had run into trouble before, and particularly in the decades after the Civil War. Those were years in which a few individuals grew immensely rich and powerful, while millions worked long hours for the meagerest kind of living wage. When workers and farmers complained and asked the goverment to do something to help them, they were told by the principal social scientists of the period, led by William Graham Sumner of Yale, that there was nothing the government could do. "The truth is," Sumner wrote, "that the social order is fixed by laws of nature precisely analogous to those of the physical order. The most that man can do . . . by his ignorance and conceit [is] to mar the operation of the social laws."

But the voices of discontent continued to cry out, and in the last quarter of the century such books as Henry George's *Progress and Poverty,* Edward Bellamy's *Looking Backward,* and William Demarest Lloyd's *Wealth versus Commonwealth* convinced millions that economic inequalities could be eliminated or at any rate reduced. At the same time a new generation of social scientists, attacking the idea of inviolable social law, argued that people were not helpless in the face of eco-

nomic disaster but could act effectively through their governments. In the first decade of the century a group of popular
journalists, known as the muckrakers, exposed special privilege
and corruption. The demand for reform grew, and in the election of 1912 two of the leading candidates, Theodore Roosevelt and Woodrow Wilson, were both reformers. Roosevelt,
calling his philosophy the New Nationalism, opposed trust-
busting, which he had previously favored, and advocated powerful business units to be balanced by powerful labor unions
and a powerful government. Wilson, calling for the New Freedom, saw government action as a way of curbing excessive
power, concentrated at that time, he believed, in the hands of
business. Both of them insisted that the government could and
should act.

The First World War interrupted Wilson's experiment in
the New Freedom, and after the war the American people
elected Warren G. Harding, who recommended a return to
normalcy. His policy was "hands off," and Big Business once
more had its own way. Since the result, on the surface at any
rate, was prosperity, the majority of the people were delighted,
and even the intellectuals, who constantly complained about
the Philistinism of a business civilization, found it pleasant
to have money in their pockets. In so far as the prosperity
of the twenties was based on new methods of mass production,
it was not only sound but revolutionary. In the spring of 1929
a liberal and far-sighted businessman, H. S. Dennison, a member of President Hoover's Committee on Economic Conditions, told me that prosperity was bound to last. Even Lincoln
Steffens, veteran of the muckraking era and admirer of Lenin's

Russia, paid tribute to the accomplishments of the New Capitalism. And then the depression began.

Although it may be that Herbert Hoover was not so indifferent to the spread of the depression as his critics have charged, his admirers can scarcely deny that his first impulse was to wait and see whether the operation of economic laws would not bring recovery. When at last he was convinced that the federal government should act, he moved slowly. Having none of his successor's gift for dramatizing his program, he became for millions of desperate people the symbol of inaction.

The New Deal was, indeed, as the learned manifesto of the Foster–Ford intellectuals called it, a mixtum compositum. Roosevelt felt that he had a mandate from the American people to do something, and he was a man to welcome such a mandate. In fifty years and more of hot debate over reforms, a vast number of ideas had been thrown up, and he and his associates seized upon those that looked feasible, without much regard for consistency. Roosevelt carried over from the Hoover administration the Reconstruction Finance Corporation and the Home Loan Banks. The National Recovery Act, with its plans for a partnership between business and government, was reminiscent of Theodore Roosevelt's New Nationalism, and, some people thought, of Mussolini's corporate state. Huge programs of public works were sanctioned by the theories of the British economist J. M. Keynes, who advocated deficit spending, or pump-priming, as it was called. The Tennessee Valley Authority had its origin in ideas about conservation, power control, and decentralization that had been debated for years in liberal circles.

In Chapter II I described the united front against the *status quo* that flourished in the twenties. So far I have been concerned with the segment of that united front that moved into the Communist orbit after the depression. But there was another and perhaps even larger segment that attached itself to the New Deal. Most of the early brain trusters had the same sort of background as the Communist intellectuals, and the young men who staffed the New Deal agencies had rubbed elbows in college liberal clubs with the young men who were talking about revolution. Spokesmen for Big Business, of course, maintained—and some have continued to maintain—that the two classes were really just alike, but history has demonstrated how significant the difference was. It is true that some Communist intellectuals infiltrated the New Deal in disguise, but that is another matter.

In point of fact, New Dealers learned from the first to distrust the Communists, and the Communists, at the outset, hated the New Deal as heartily as did Big Business. To the Marxist it was obvious that the New Deal couldn't work because it was based on an incorrect theory of the crisis, or, more accurately, on no theory at all. (It was a Marxist, though not a Stalinist, who said in 1935, "There is nothing the New Deal has so far done that could not have been done better by an earthquake.") At best, we felt, it could merely postpone the collapse of capitalism. By 1935, however, we had to admit that the New Deal had substantially reduced the sufferings caused by the depression and the great majority of the American people favored it. Some of us were also beginning to see that without the New Deal we might have had, not a Communist, but a fascist revolution. When the party line changed,

so as to permit qualified support of the New Deal, I was delighted. Now I could eat my cake and have it too.

Actually what I and other Marxists thought of as the weakness of the New Deal was its strength. That is, it was strong
because it was not based on a theory or dogma. The New Deal's
only dogma was the principle forged in fifty years of reform
agitation—that the federal government could and should do
whatever was necessary to guarantee the economic well-being
of the people. In its choice of means it was flexible, and often
erratic. But when Roosevelt made mistakes, and he made
plenty, he was able and willing to abandon them and start
over again. He didn't ask whether a plan was correct according
to this theory or that; he simply found out whether or not
it would work.

In *The Big Change* Frederick Lewis Allen maintains that
we have evolved in this country a new kind of economic system, which he speaks of as "beyond socialism." When I wrote
I Like America in 1938, I drew upon various statistical surveys
to prove that this country could produce vastly more than it
was producing, could produce enough for everybody. But, I
argued, those possibilities could be realized only if production were freed from the fetters put upon it by Big Business—
could be realized, in other words, only through socialism. Now
it turns out that these estimates of America's productive
capacity were ridiculously low. During the war our production
of military goods alone surpassed these guesses, and still the
standard of living went up and up. After the Korean crisis
of 1950, we again began producing huge amounts of military
goods, and the standard of living continued to rise. And all
this was done without benefit of socialism.

Our achievements, in fact, make the most romantic promises of the Socialists and Communists look silly. Not only are we producing more goods than anybody fifteen years ago dreamed of; we are doing better and better with distribution. In 1948, according to statistics quoted by Mr. Allen, more than 70 per cent of American families had incomes between $2000 and $10,000 a year. Only 3 per cent had more than $10,000, and only 10.6 per cent had less than $1000. Needless to say, this is not a perfect state of affairs, but when you look back, not to the depths of the depression but to the prosperous twenties, it sounds wonderful.

How did it all come about? Not simply by virtue of the New Deal. To begin with, it was made possible by our great natural resources. Then there is the fact that the industrial revolution got an early start in America, earlier than anywhere else except in Great Britain. More important, the second industrial revolution—the development of mass production—began in this country. We had the essentials—raw materials, a large population, engineering skill—and we created what was talked about in the late twenties as the New Capitalism: a capitalism that was interested in the wider distribution of wealth for the sake of larger markets, a capitalism in which management counted for more than ownership.

But the New Capitalism, as Lincoln Steffens said, went over the top and down into the abyss. To Steffens, as to many others, this seemed to prove that capitalism was finished, but the New Dealers were determined to see what reforms and modifications would do. While Big Business charged that the New Deal was seeking to destroy the capitalist system, we Communists maintained that it was making a futile effort to keep the system going. In the main we were nearer right than Big Business, but we were wrong about the futility of the effort. Capitalism as modified by New Deal measures showed a vitality that made nonsense of Marxist predictions.

All this was not accomplished without a tremendous struggle, in the polling places and in Congress and in the factories as well. If generations of reformers had prepared the way for the New Deal, so had generations of militant working men. With the National Labor Relations Act, the labor-union movement won the recognition for which it had been fighting for more than a century. The important mass industries—automobiles, rubber, textiles, steel—were mostly unorganized before the NLRA was passed. Now the CIO moved into these fields, and the labor movement became a great economic and political force. It became, indeed, an integral and indispensable part of our productive system.

Although everyone knows that there are many abuses in the labor movement, most people realize that we could not get along without the unions. The vast, impersonal units of mass production would crush the individual worker if he stood alone. The responsible unions not only protect the economic well-being of their members; they preserve their self-respect, and they enrich their lives in many ways. (Take a look, for instance, at Unity House, the great summer resort in the Poconos owned by the International Ladies Garment Workers Union.) They also simplify the tasks of management, and many a businessman who fought unionization has come to regard the unions as an asset. Finally, the unions are an instrument for achieving a constantly rising standard of living, and this is essential to high productivity.

Nobody knows exactly what it is we have got—some people call it a mixed economy—but at any rate it seems to work. Certainly it is not the laissez-faire capitalism of the Manchester liberals, for business is curbed in many directions by government regulation and in others by the strength of organized labor. On the other hand, it isn't socialism, for most of the means of production are privately owned, and the profit motive is still important. So long as it works, however, nobody cares about the name.

Admittedly we have no guarantee that it will go on working. We have been living for thirteen or fourteen years in a war economy, and we do not know what would happen if large expenditures for military purposes should cease to be necessary, nor do we know how long we can go on making such expenditures. But a few things have been made clear. First, Marxist dogmas have been proved false. Instead of the rich getting richer and the poor getting poorer, there has been a remarkable leveling off of income, and Big Business, however reluctantly, has accepted government regulation. Second, there seems little likelihood that the lessons of the great depression will be forgotten. A Republican administration has given business a freer hand than it had, but President Eisenhower has warned that the full powers of the government will be used in case of economic crisis. Finally, the limits of our productive capacity are nowhere near in sight, and the standard of living can go higher and higher.

There is plenty to worry about, especially the possibility— the probability—of atomic war, in the course of which everything we have achieved might be wiped out. And even apart from this terrifying danger, the state of the nation does not warrant complacence. There are still many gross injustices and inequalities. Moreover, material prosperity, important as it is, leaves many problems unsolved, and a man would have to be blind to say that we are doing as well morally and culturally as we are economically.

Yet, when every possible allowance is made, the superiority of life in America to life in Russia is beyond dispute. To begin with, we have beaten the Communists at what is supposed to be their own game: not only are we ahead of them in production, we have come closer to their stated ideal of equality. The facts about real incomes in Russia are hard to come by, but careful students, working with Russian sources, have concluded that the privileged classes in Russia—the party leaders, important bureaucrats, high army officers, etc.—receive incomes a hundred times greater than those of ordinary workers. The great mass of the Russian people are found at the bottom of the economic pyramid, whereas our largest group, as we have seen, is in the middle brackets, with only a few above and no great number below.

The average American citizen is prosperous and free; the average Russian citizen is poor and a slave. No one knows how many Russians have died because they were displeasing to the government. If we include the peasants who were starved to death by the government's agricultural policy in 1932–33, the number runs into the millions. Nor is there any telling how many are in slave-labor camps today, though again we know that it is in the millions that the figure must be calculated. For years now we have read in the Communist press about an endless series of trials, purges, and deportations. That a revolution should bring a reign of terror is something for which history had prepared us; that the terror should be steadily intensified over a period of thirty-five years reminds us that history sometimes does not repeat but outdoes itself. When, soon after the death of Stalin, one of his three successors, Lavrenti Beria, was purged, the pattern of terror was exposed for everyone to see.

The blindest Soviet sympathizer cannot maintain that there is political freedom in Russia or the satellites; the operations of the one-party system are revealed every time there is a so-called election. Nor can anyone argue that there is freedom of speech, when biologists, philologists, literary critics, historians—scholars of every kind—are constantly being purged for deviations from the party line. According to Bertram Wolfe, Stalin's picture appeared on the front page of every issue of *Pravda* and *Izvestia,* the leading Russian newspapers, for a period of years; and the unanimity with which the papers denounced Beria after his arrest demonstrated that Stalin's death had not resulted in freedom of the press. It is said again and again; it is a commonplace; but it is true—there is no freedom in Russia.

Freedom is not to be taken for granted in America. There have always been people who thought that other people ought to conform to their ideas, and today the people who want conformity are on the one hand frightened by Communism, and on the other emboldened by the strength of anti-Communism. It gets said more and more openly that so-and-so may not be a Communist but is, in this way or that, undependable or "controversial." It is not enough, we hear, to fight Communism; we must uproot the ideas out of which Communism grows—which may be any ideas the speaker happens to disagree with.

This is dangerous business and must be taken seriously, but we ought not to conclude that freedom is dead in the United States. Dissent is sometimes penalized in ways that it shouldn't be, but it is possible. Many unpopular ideas, including open and avowed Communism, do get expressed in speech and in print, and if there are people who are scared to speak out, there are others who aren't. I don't want to seem to defend in any way the punishment of dissent, but I must point out that dissent has been punished before and that truth has survived.

Democracy is a going concern in the United States. Needless to say, we do not have perfect democracy; in a society as complicated as ours it is impossible for everybody to take an equal share in administering the government. Ours is simply a rough-and-ready democracy, a method of conducting the business of society that serves the interests of the majority of the people, not as somebody else conceives those interests but as the people themselves do. Special privilege has not been eliminated, but machinery does exist by which it can be combated. Basic human rights are protected in theory and most of the time in practice. The fact that our rough-and-ready democracy is still functioning, after two world wars and a great depression, encourages us to believe that it can survive the extended struggle, cold or hot, against Communism. The essence of democracy is the ability to delegate power without surrendering freedom. We have had to delegate vast powers to our government in the modern era, and freedom has not perished.

There are two conclusions to be drawn at the present time, and perhaps some others to be drawn later on. The first of the present conclusions is the obvious one: what we have in this country is worth defending, not only because we have a higher standard of living and an infinitely more decent form of government than Russia has, and not only because we like our way of life and do not intend to let anyone impose a different way upon us, but also because we have come closer than any other nation to abolishing poverty. What we defend is, among other things, a great human achievement. And then, in the second place, it seems clear that the well-being of the American people makes us a strong nation. The spirit in which we carry on our struggle should not be the spirit of fear.

VIII

Shall We Investigate?

The traditional man from Mars, reading our newspapers, would surely get the impression that the weapon on which we put most reliance in the struggle against Communism is the legislative inquiry. I am afraid that many Americans have the same idea. And why not, with three Congressional committees and heaven knows how many state committees competing for headlines?

My own experience with legislative investigations into subversion began in the summer of 1948, when I went to Seattle to lecture at the Pacific Northwest Writers' Conference. In the lobby of my hotel, on the first morning of the conference, I was handed a subpoena, which stated that I was "commanded to appear and attend before the Joint Legislative Fact-Finding Committee on Un-American Activities" and "there to remain until discharged by said committee." Since I had crossed the continent to deliver a series of lectures, I was dismayed at the prospect of spending the week—and perhaps weeks to come—at the 146th Field Artillery Armory, but the young man who had served the subpoena explained that it was merely a formality. "Mr. Houston wants to talk to you," he said. "He'll call you up." Then the young man vanished and I hurried to my first lecture.

Before arriving in Seattle, I had never heard of this committee, commonly known as the Canwell committee, but in the few hours since my arrival I had learned, from the papers and from my hosts, that a full-scale investigation of Communism at the University of Washington was beginning on the same day as the writers' conference. The hearings continued for five days, just as the conference did, and they brought out the information that three members of the faculty had belonged to the Communist party but had resigned, that two were currently party members, and that one man had a long record of affiliation with party fronts. The case of the six was investigated by the university administration, and the following January the three ex-members were put on probation and the other three were dismissed.

So much for what the Canwell committee accomplished, without, as it happened, any help from me. On the second day of the hearings I was summoned to meet Mr. Houston at the Seattle Athletic Club, where, I discovered, the Canwell committee was giving a banquet for the Tolland committee, its opposite number in California. While the members of the two committees, their wives, and various guests were warming up, I sat in a corner, talking to Mr. Houston, the Canwell committee's chief investigator.

When I told Mr. Houston that I knew nothing whatever about Communism on the campus of the University of Washington, he admitted that this was probably true but suggested that I might have something to say about the general menace of Communism in education. I knew what he meant. During the first two days of the hearings, two imported witnesses had testified: J. B. Matthews, once chief investigator for the Dies committee, and Howard Rushmore, an ex-Communist who was currently writing for the Hearst newspapers. These witnesses, both of whom were to turn up five years later on the staff of Senator Joseph McCarthy, had given a horrendous account of Communist influence in the nation's universities, Matthews having suggested, among other things, that the new president of Columbia, Dwight D. Eisenhower, was by no means above suspicion. If Mr. Houston could get me to take the stand and add even a few mild details, he might strengthen his case, and there would certainly be more headlines.

I had no craving for that kind of publicity and no desire to help Mr. Houston. What was necessary, I saw, was to convince him that I would not be a useful witness, while being careful not to antagonize him to such an extent that he would put me on the stand anyway, just to get even. We talked for quite a long time, while all around us the party was getting larger and louder, and at last I reminded him that I had to deliver an evening lecture. He was a little tough right at the end, hinting that maybe I would be seeing him again, but, as I learned the next day, he immediately told a member of the committee that he was not going to call me.

I had begun the interview with a strong determination that I was not going to testify if I could help it. What I had read about the investigation had convinced me that it was being conducted with little consideration for the rights of those being questioned, and it was clear to me that some innocent men and women were being made to suffer, along with some who were probably guilty of being Communists. If, however, I had had any notion of testifying, that banquet would have knocked it out of me. Here were two sets of legislative Red-

hunters in a relaxed mood—out on a spree, in fact—and it was
not a reassuring spectacle. I don't mean that there was anything sinister about the members of the Canwell and Tolland
committees. On the contrary, they were just run-of-the-mill
state legislators, feeling virtuous because, as one Washington
representative said in proposing a toast to a California representative, they were fighting the good fight, and also feeling
happy because they were in on a good thing, politically speaking. (It didn't turn out to be so good for Representative Canwell and Senator Bienz, co-chairmen of the committee, for
both failed of re-election the next November.) But obviously
they were neither subtle enough to fight Communism intelli-
gently, nor wise enough to protect the innocent, and I had no
doubt that they would do more harm than good.

The sequel to their investigation of the University of Washington seems to prove that I was right. Three men lost their
jobs, and three others were put in a humiliating position that
must have made effective teaching almost impossible. The
university inquiry that followed the Canwell committee's
hearings went on for many weeks, and during this whole
period, if one can judge from the university newspaper, the
student body was in an uproar. Some apparently innocent
men and women were besmirched, and others must have been
badly frightened. A lot of damage was done, and, on the other
hand, all that was accomplished was the dismissal of one associate professor of psychology, one assistant professor of philosophy, and an associate in English. All had been members
of the faculty for twenty years or more, and although their
political sympathies, if not their party affiliation, had been
well known, no evidence was produced of subversive teaching.

To anyone with academic experience it is significant that, although Gundlach, Phillips, and Butterworth had been connected with the university for many years, none of them had achieved the rank of full professor. This, it seems probable, was because their political sympathies were so well known: the university would not fire them, but it would not promote them. Then the Canwell committee, appealing to the widespread fear and hatred of Communism, worked up a hysterical conviction that the university was overrun with subversives, and was able to produce two bona fide party members, one likely suspect, and three ex-members. President Allen had no choice but to refer the six cases to the Faculty Committee on Tenure and Academic Freedom, which held hearings for seven weeks. The committee voted seven to four for the dismissal of Gundlach, partly on the ground that he had been evasive in his testimony, and eight to three for the retention of Phillips and Butterworth, who had admitted that they were party members. President Allen, however, recommended to the regents the dismissal of all three, and his recommendation was followed.

Even if one is perfectly convinced, as I am not, that a Communist teacher is at all times and in all circumstances a danger, it does seem clear that the problem was handled at the University of Washington in a highly undesirable fashion. One gathers that many people in the State of Washington, once they had a chance to cool off, came to that conclusion, since they refused to send Canwell and Bienz back to the legislature.

Legislative inquiries into subversion have been going on more or less continuously for the past thirty-five years. In 1919 the New York State legislature appointed a joint committee "to investigate the scope, tendencies, and ramifications of such seditious activities." This committee, known as the Lusk committee, after its chairman, Clayton R. Lusk, came up in 1920 with a four-volume report, each volume running to more than a thousand pages. It also cooperated in a series of raids, leading to the arrest of several hundred persons on suspicion of "criminal anarchy."

Volumes III and IV of the Lusk report, "Constructive Movements," are dull reading, but Volumes I and II, "Destructive Movements," are full of interest and value for the social historian. The committee's researchers were well trained, and their histories of the Socialist party, the Socialist Labor party, the Communist party, the Communist Labor party, the Industrial Workers of the World, etc., are essentially reliable. The volumes also include many important documents regarding the rise of the Bolshevik party in Russia, the October Revolution, and the founding of the Third International.

As one proceeds, however, one realizes how wide a net the committee was throwing out. It investigated the Amalgamated Clothing Workers of America, the International Ladies Garment Workers Union, and a number of other unions, all of which it found under influences that were, by its definition, subversive. It maintained that organizations for the establishment and maintenance of peace were as dangerous as organizations that publicly proclaimed their intention of overthrowing the government. Subversive propaganda, it discovered, was rampant both in the colleges and in the churches.

If you will glance at the index of the report, you will see that the Lusk committee regarded as subversive many of the

most distinguished men and women in America. Here on the first page is the name of Jane Addams, founder of the famous Hull House in Chicago: Miss Addams was "chairman, National Woman's Peace Party," "member, American Civil Liberties Union," "member, Fellowship of Reconciliation," etc., etc. Looking up these organizations, you find that they either preached criminal anarchy themselves or had members who belonged to organizations that did. As you go on, your eye catches one familiar name after another. What did A. A. Berle do? He was a member of the executive committee of the American Civil Liberties Union. The Reverend Henry Sloane Coffin? He had protested against the Espionage Act. Herbert Croly, who had been a great friend of Theodore Roosevelt? He was an editor of the *New Republic* and a member of the Bureau for Industrial Research. Professor John Dewey was "member 'I.W.W.' defense committee." (This was a committee, with such members as Thorstein Veblen, Helen Keller, and James Harvey Robinson, that had raised funds to see that a group of Wobblies arrested in Chicago had competent defense lawyers.) Clarence Darrow? "Relations with Civil Liberties Bureau." Professor Richard T. Ely? "Activities in 'Christian Socialist' movement." William T. Russell, Catholic bishop of Charleston? "Leaning toward Socialism." Professor John K. Ryan of Catholic University? "Leaning toward Socialism." The Reverend Franklin S. Spaulding, an Episcopal clergyman? "Opposed to 'industrialism' and 'nationalism.' "
Here are a few more of the Lusk committee's subversives: Professor Irving Fisher, Zona Gale, Professor N. S. B. Gras, Professor Carlton J. Hayes, the Reverend Bernard Iddings Bell, Senator Robert LaFollette, Judge Ben B. Lindsey, Pro-

fessor Harry A. Overstreet, George Foster Peabody, Carl Sandburg, and Ordway Tead.

The case of Ordway Tead, who was to serve for many years as chairman of the Board of Higher Education of New York City, is instructive. His crime was the fact that he was a member of the Bureau of Industrial Research. And what was this bureau? I quote the report in full:

A so-called Bureau of Industrial Research, established at West 23rd Street, New York City, describes itself as being "organized to promote sound human relationships in industry." In addition to the courses in employment administration, the bureau offers expert industrial counsel and technical assistance to employers and trade-union executives. Its research department maintains a library of current information covering the field of industrial relations, from which it is prepared to supply documentary and statistical data at moderate cost to individuals, corporations, labor organizations, and the press.

Its director is Robert W. Bruere; its treasurer, Herbert Crowley [sic] of the "New Republic." Its other members are Ordway Tead, Henry C. Metcalf, P. Sargent Florence, Leonard Outhwaite, Carl G. Karsten, Mary D. Blankenhorn.

It also has special lecturers: John A. Fitch and Irwin H. Schell.

This organization cooperates with the "New School for Social Research," which has been established by men who belong to the ranks of the near-Bolshevik intelligentsia, some of them being too radical in their views to remain on the faculty of Columbia University.

The passage appears in a section of the report headed "Socialist Propaganda in Educated Circles" and in a chapter with the title, "Academic and Scholastic Socialist Activities."

The pay-off, of course, is in the last paragraph: the only thing the committee has against the bureau is that it "cooperates" —we are not told how—with the New School for Social Research. And what was the committee's case against the New School? We don't precisely know, for there is no discussion in the report of the New School as such—a curious omission if it was held to be a dangerously subversive institution. The charge made here, that it was "established by men who belong to the ranks of the near-Bolshevik intelligentsia," is never substantiated in any way. The only other reference to the New School comes in a passage on the dismissal from the Columbia University faculty of Professor H. W. L. Dana, "on account of his pacifist activities." "This was followed," the report continues, "by the withdrawal from the Columbia faculty of Professors Charles A. Beard and Henry R. Mussey, both of whom became active in radical teachings, especially in connection with the New School for Social Research." Note that Beard and Mussey were not fired, as seems to be implied in the passage quoted earlier, and note that they resigned, not because they were "too radical in their views," but in protest against what they regarded as a violation of academic freedom. The report, incidentally, lists no examples of radical activity under Beard's name and accuses Mussey only of serving on the executive committee of the Civil Liberties Bureau. Yet Ordway Tead was listed as a subversive because an organization to which he belonged "cooperated" with an organization to which Beard and Mussey belonged. Can one ask for a more perfect example of what we have learned to call "guilt by association"?

You cannot read far in the Lusk report without realizing

that the committee regarded any criticism of the *status quo* as ground for suspicion. It investigated not only Communists and anarchists and others who might be regarded as revolutionaries but also Christian Socialists, pacifists, single-taxers, and trade unionists. In short, it opposed every kind of dissent. Thus it fell into disrepute with most Americans who were capable of independent thinking.

There is another reason why legislative investigations came to be looked upon as dangerous, and that is the fact that they contributed to, if they did not cause, the mood of hysteria that prevailed in the years after World War I. Early in 1919 a committee of the United States Senate, commonly known as the Overman committee, transferred its attentions from German propaganda, which had become old hat, to Bolshevik propaganda. A young American journalist and poet, John Reed, who had been in Russia during the revolution, and had been converted to Communism, asked (how times have changed!) to be allowed to appear before the committee. After he had testified, a Florida newspaper published an editorial entitled, "One Man Who Needs the Rope";

John Reed told the Senate committee investigating Bolshevism that he was a firm advocate of revolution in the United States. . . . If there is no law for handling a case of this kind one should be enacted speedily. If a man should be hanged for instigating another to murder one man, he should certainly be hanged for instigating men to kill thousands of men. If the law is defective, why wait until tomorrow to remedy its defects? A law should be passed at once against such utterances as those brazenly made by this man Reed, and then as soon as possible ten thousand hangings should follow.

There were not, fortunately, ten thousand hangings, but while the country was in this mood some of the most disgraceful episodes in our history took place. States and cities hysterically passed laws restricting freedom of speech and assembly. Returning soldiers rioted against Bolsheviks, who as often as not turned out to be ordinary working people who were trying to form a union, or respectable middle-aged ladies who were in favor of peace. Attorney General A. Mitchell Palmer arrested more than four thousand persons, whom he charged with being alien Communists. Many radicals were beaten by mobs, and some were lynched.

Inevitably the hysteria was turned against the labor movement. Organized labor had gained in strength during the war, and it had done its patriotic duty. Once the war was over, labor leaders felt that the time had come for shorter hours and higher pay, and a series of strikes developed, including a great strike in the steel industry against the twelve-hour day. All strikers were denounced as Bolsheviks, and not only were the sentiments of right-thinking citizens rallied against them but Attorney General Palmer was generous with injunctions against picketing. According to Frederick Lewis Allen, in *Only Yesterday*, the American businessman "had come out of the war with a militant patriotism; and mingling his idealistic with his selfish motives, after the manner of all men at all times, he developed a fervent belief that 100-per-cent Americanism and the Welfare of God's Own Country and Loyalty to the Teachings of the Founding Fathers implied the right of the businessman to kick the union organizer out of his workshop." Anyone who didn't agree was likely to be called a Bolshevik.

Gradually, as the war slipped into the past and as America entered the period of the great boom, the country grew calmer. Legislative inquiries did not thrive in the later twenties and early thirties, but there were certain individuals, often described as "professional patriots," who were determined to prove that the nation was in acute peril from the Bolshevik conspiracy: S. Stanwood Menken of the National Security League, Ralph Easley of the National Civic Federation, E. H. Hunter of the Industrial Defense Association, and others. By using the principle of guilt by association, they undertook to prove that there were hundreds of thousands of Communists in America, with a vast influence, but most people laughed at their exaggerations.

All this explains why the House Committee on Un-American Activities, when it was brought into being in May 1938, was widely regarded as a bad joke. Certainly we Communists and our close sympathizers were eager to discredit this committee, not, however, because we were afraid that it would have any serious effect on our activities, but because we saw that we could make common cause against it with non-Communist liberals and thus win allies. And Martin Dies played beautifully into our hands. In the first place, although the committee was supposed to investigate not only pro-Communist but also pro-Fascist activities, it devoted four or five times as much energy to the former as to the latter, and this at a time when fascism was on the march in Europe. In the second place, it adopted the techniques—exaggeration and guilt by association—that the liberals had learned to expect from the professional patriots. And in the third place, Representative Dies made it quite clear that he was interested in exposing not only the Communists but also everyone who disagreed with his views on economics. In his book, *The Trojan Horse in America,* he wrote: "The Fifth Column and the Trojan Horse organizations can never be properly dealt with so long as we retain in the Government service—even in its key positions—hundreds of Left-wingers and radicals who do not believe in our system of private enterprise. . . . These Left-wingers . . . do not understand that liberty and the Bill of Rights cannot survive the destruction of the American economic system." Said the non-Communist liberals, "Look who's talking about the Bill of Rights!"

From the Lusk committee to the Dies committee, legislative inquiries into subversion, whether on a state or a national basis, seemed foolish and futile. But after World War II, when the Soviet Union turned aggressive and directed its hostility against the United States, the situation changed. Since Communists were actual or potential agents of the enemy, something had to be done. As a matter of fact, the Federal Bureau of Investigation and other intelligence agencies had been on the alert all along, but their work, in order to be done efficiently, had to be done quietly. The public wanted to be reassured; they wanted to know that Communists were being hunted down. In this atmosphere legislative investigations began to flourish. State committees were created or reactivated, and the House Committee on Un-American Activities became more vigorous and more esteemed. The Senate entered the field with its Subcommittee on Internal Security, headed first by Senator McCarran and, after the Republicans took over Congress, by Senator Jenner. But it was not Representative (later Vice-President) Nixon nor Representative Velde nor Senator McCarran nor Senator Jenner who was to satisfy the public demand for a Great Investigator; that role was to be assumed by Senator Joseph McCarthy of Wisconsin.

To many Americans today Senator McCarthy is the perfect symbol of true patriotism, and anyone who criticizes him is what my local newspaper calls "a Red or a pinko or a sympathizer." To other Americans, however, and to millions of people in the European democracies, he is a dangerous demagogue. The critics of McCarthy, it seems to me, often exaggerate the damage that he has done and is capable of doing, but the fact remains that he is much more a demagogue than he is a patriot. To follow his career is to learn a great deal about how not to fight Communism.

When he entered the Senate in 1947, Joseph McCarthy was simply a tough, ambitious politician whose record was full of question marks. More than most people, he didn't care how he got what he wanted so long as he got it, and he had a lot of nerve. In Wisconsin he had never been known as an anti-Communist, nor did he distinguish himself as an enemy of the Reds during his first three years in the Senate. On February 9, 1950, however, speaking to a Women's Republican Club in Wheeling, West Virginia, he said, "I have here in my hand a list of two hundred and five . . . a list of names that were made known to the Secretary of State as being members of the Communist Party and who nevertheless are still working and shaping policy in the State Department." The speech made headlines, and the career of the Great Investigator had been launched.

The number of Communists that McCarthy had found in the State Department was sometimes two hundred and five, sometimes eighty-one, sometimes fifty-seven. Actually he has never named a single member of the Communist party who was working for the State Department on February 9, 1950. The only charge that came anywhere near to sticking was that made against Owen Lattimore, who, though never a member of the State Department, had served in advisory capacities at various times. Even here, however, McCarthy's charge was wide of the mark, for he had asserted that Lattimore was "the top espionage agent in the United States," and yet neither he nor any of the witnesses before the McCarran committee produced any evidence of espionage. It is significant that in the indictment of Lattimore for perjury there was no mention of espionage or of membership in the Communist party.

If one can imagine McCarthy's compiling a Handbook for Demagogues, the first maxim in it would certainly be "Some mud always sticks." That was the lesson of the Wheeling speech, and it is one that he has never forgotten. The second maxim would be "Names make news." In a speech before the Senate in June 1951 he stated that General George C. Marshall, as Chief of Staff and as Secretary of Defense, had helped Russia, and was either a dupe or a traitor. He was a man "whose every important act for years has contributed to the prosperity of the enemy," part of a "conspiracy so immense and an infamy so black as to dwarf any previous such venture in the history of man." Newspapers throughout the country might denounce these charges editorially as criminally irresponsible, but they had to print them on their front pages.

Between 1950 and 1953, however, McCarthy was merely

warming up. It was after his re-election, and after the election
of an administration that had not repudiated his support, that
he took the center of the stage as the Great Investigator. His
third maxim could now be formulated: "The public has a
short memory." He opened up with an attack on the Voice of
America that virtually paralyzed it at a time when, because of
the death of Stalin and the subsequent disorders in satellite
countries, psychological warfare was of the highest importance.
Quickly he went on to investigate the overseas libraries of
the United States Information Service, and was able to achieve
the burning of a few books. Simultaneously he led the Senate
fight against the confirmation of Charles Bohlen as Ambas-
sador to Moscow, suggesting at one point that Mr. Bohlen
ought to be given a test with a lie detector. ("Now tell me,
Ken," I heard him say a few weeks later on a radio program
with Kenneth Crawford, "when did I ever smear anybody?")
He also took time to tangle with James Wechsler, editor of the
New York *Post,* whom he charged with following the party
line—the only apparent evidence being the fact that Wechsler
had criticized McCarthy.

McCarthy's rapid shifting from one target to another not
only served to keep his name in the headlines; it obscured the
fact that his investigations rarely produced results. (The
public does have a short memory.) His audacity seemed to
have no bounds. When he wasn't promising a startling new
revelation, he was intimating that Charles Bohlen was a liar
or telling James B. Conant that he wasn't fit to be High Com-
missioner of Germany. He never did subpoena former President Truman, but his threat to do so got top billing. (Names
do make news.) And again and again one would read in the

pro-McCarthy press that so-and-so had been discredited, even though McCarthy's charges had never been substantiated in any way. (Some mud always sticks.)

As I write these pages,[1] Senator McCarthy is less than twenty-five miles away, for he has charged up to Albany to investigate subversion in the General Electric plant in Schenectady. In recent months he has swept through the Government Printing Office, tangled with the Army over his release of a restricted pamphlet, rushed back from his honeymoon to expose some "extremely dangerous espionage" at the Fort Monmouth radar laboratories, and given President Pusey advice on the running of Harvard University.

There is no denying the fact that he puts on an exceedingly good show, and it is to his showmanship that much of his popularity can be attributed. I myself, at times when his reputation seemed to be slipping, have felt that life would be rather dull without him. On the other hand, I am not foolish enough to underestimate the damage he has done. Scores and probably hundreds of persons have lost their jobs as a result of his activities, and yet there apparently has not been evidence enough against a single one of these persons to warrant indictment for espionage or any other crime. Protected by Congressional immunity, he has besmirched the reputations of some of our most eminent citizens, and he has bullied and insulted dozens of witnesses before his committee. His disregard for truth, for justice, and for human decency has made all previous investigators seem like Solons and Daniels.

[1] Obviously it is impossible to keep up with McCarthy in a book; a daily newspaper can scarcely do the job; what one needs is an every-hour-on-the-hour broadcast.

And, far from being an effective enemy of Communism, he has been its greatest asset. Herbert Philbrick, who spent nine years in the Communist party as a counterspy for the FBI, has written: "According to leaders of the Communist party, McCarthy has helped them a great deal. The kind of attacks he has made do three things that the comrades like: They add greatly to the confusion, putting up a smokescreen for the party and making it more difficult than ever for people to discern just who is a Communist and who is not; they make the party appear a lot stronger than it is; and they do considerable damage to the 'stupid liberal' whom the party hates." It may be added that McCarthyism is today almost the only basis on which the party can win sympathizers.

But, it will be said, legislative inquiries are not necessarily bad just because McCarthy is a dangerous character, and that is true. Investigating committees constitute one of the important instruments of democracy. Not only do they provide a basis for legislation, which is supposed to be their function; they serve to educate the public, and they are often a way of getting things done. Since the American people are much concerned with Communism, and rightly so, it seems only natural that their representatives should investigate the problem.

The theory is fine, but, as this chapter suggests, there are difficulties and dangers in putting it into practice. Defenders of the Congressional investigations point out that liberals never get excited about investigations into gambling or tax scandals but reserve their indignation for inquiries into Communism. The implication is, of course, that the liberals want to protect the Communists, and of some self-styled liberals, whom I discuss in detail later on, this may be true. However, as the apologists for Messrs. Velde, Jenner, and Mc-Carthy never seem to realize, bona fide liberals with no interest in helping the Communists have special reasons for scrutinizing this type of inquiry. Communism is, among other things, a set of ideas, and the political investigation of ideas is always dangerous.

What the dangers are has already been indicated. The Lusk committee, supposedly investigating "criminal anarchy," pointed an accusing finger at all unorthodox ideas in politics and economics. Martin Dies was perhaps more concerned with attacking the New Deal than with exposing Communism. Senator McCarthy wants to purge from the government not only the Communists but also those he calls "Communist-minded," a term that includes anyone who disagrees with him. Legislative investigations of Communism have almost always turned out to be heresy-hunts.

Defenders of the inquiries know this as well as anyone else, and they simply don't care. They, too, dislike New Dealers, members of the Keynesian school of economics, advocates of the TVA, etc., and they are perfectly willing to have them suffer. Now there is no reason why anyone shouldn't say that the New Deal was a calamity, or that any departure from the economics of Adam Smith is a step on the road to slavery, or that the TVA is creeping socialism. That is freedom of speech. People can say these things and do their best to convince other people of their truth. But when the power of the government is used to penalize Keynesians, let us say, freedom of speech is imperiled. If I choose to say that the world is flat, I am going to expose myself to considerable abuse, but that is quite all right; the man who abuses me is exercising the same right as I am. But when my name appears on an official government list of subversives, that is something else.

To serve its proper purpose, a legislative investigation of Communism would have to be discriminating in a high degree; the investigators would have to know exactly what they were doing and be firmly resolved not to do anything else. The conditions of practical politics, however, make such discrimination virtually impossible. When liberals say this, they are immediately charged with being undemocratic or with desiring a government of the elite. Actually they are guilty of nothing but realism. Democracy functions by way of politicians, and politicians are necessarily concerned with political ends. No legislator would accept membership on an investigating committee without considering how it affected his political chances, and only the exceptional legislator would pass up opportunities for furthering his ambitions. So consistent an opportunism as Joseph McCarthy's may be exceptional, but opportunism is an essential element in political success. These are facts that we have to accept, and there is no sense in quarreling with them. This is how our government operates, and if it isn't perfect, it is infinitely preferable to anything that exists in the totalitarian countries. Yet we may well hesitate before entrusting to the products of this rough-and-ready system the delicate task of investigating ideas.

When I was summoned to testify before the House Committee on Un-American Activities on February 25, 1953, the committee as organized under the new Republican administration was holding its first public hearings, and, as I have said, its members were obviously determined to be fair in their treatment of witnesses. I would be the last to suggest that Chairman Velde was indifferent to the publicity and hence to the political value of his position, but it seemed to me that he and the other members of the committee were trying to do a conscientious job. Three of us—Robert Gorham Davis, Daniel Boorstin, and I—were appearing as so-called cooperative witnesses, but the fourth witness, Wendell Furry, was uncooperative, and even he was treated for the most part with courtesy and restraint. There was none of the bulldozing and abuse to which witnesses before Senator McCarthy's committee, and other committees, too, have frequently been subjected. But, as I asked at the end of my testimony, how much had the two days of investigation accomplished? It had been proved that there were a dozen or so Communists at Harvard University fourteen years ago, and it had been indicated that there might be one there at the present time. (Professor Furry subsequently satisfied the administration of the university that he had left the party in 1947.) Was that anything to get excited about?

The pragmatic test is the one we have to apply: how much good and how much harm do legislative inquiries into Communism actually do? They have led to the dismissal of a good many hundred persons from their jobs as teachers, government employees, movie and radio script writers, etc., and there is not much doubt in my mind that a large proportion of these persons were or recently had been members of the Communist party. Whether it is always a good thing for a Communist to lose his job is a question, but let us assume for the moment that it is. We can then give the investigations credit for reducing the power and influence of Communism in this country, which is in itself desirable. On the other hand, it must be granted that the investigations have not been very successful in striking at those forms of Communist activity— espionage and sabotage—that are most dangerous to the national security. The Committee on Un-American Activities did expose the existence of the spy ring of which Alger Hiss was a member, but that was in the past. So far as spies have been caught, they have been caught by the FBI.

Against this rather dubious record of achievement stands a clear record of damage done. I have already spoken of the extent to which freedom of speech is menaced by these investigations, and I have touched, in speaking of Senator McCarthy, on the perils of hysteria. With three investigating committees going full blast, each of them eager to make headlines, the newspapers inevitably give the impression that the country is overrun with Communists. Again we have to take into account the realities of contemporary life, one of which is that most newspaper readers like to be shocked by sensational headlines. Except for a handful of large metropolitan dailies, the newspapers, in reporting on the hearings in which I took part, paid no attention to Mr. Davis's admirable analysis of the factors that led to the growth of Communism in the thirties, nor did they repeat my suggestion that the emphasis should fall on how little Communism there was rather than how much. No, they concentrated on the recalcitrant witness, Dr. Furry, and said of Mr. Davis and me only that we had identified him as a Communist.

One has only to go through the experience of testifying to realize that these inquiries cannot fail to leave a false im-

pression on the public mind. On March 9, 1953, the Troy
Record quoted our local Congressman, Dean Taylor, as saying, "If, for instance, there are twenty-one members of the
Harvard University faculty, then certainly it is an indication
of infiltration into the institutions of higher learning." Now
Mr. Davis had mentioned twenty-one educators known to him
to be Communists, but a number of them were not teaching
at Harvard. He and I and Mr. Boorstin agreed that there had
been about twelve members of our party branch in 1938–39.
Furthermore, and this is the real point, that was fourteen
years ago. Testimony, as I have already said, indicated that
there was only one Communist currently at Harvard, and he
turned out to be an ex-Communist. When I wrote about this
to Mr. Taylor, he quoted from a garbled newspaper story
and went on to say that he himself had been misquoted.

If one were to take into account only the way in which the
public mind is misled and kept in agitation by these inquiries,
it would seem probable that the harm that is done outweighs
the good, but there is also the question of the damage that is
done to a large—and today rapidly increasing—number of
persons. That, however, is a theme for another chapter.

IX

People Get Hurt

At the close of my testimony before the House Committee on Un-American Activities, one of the members, Representative Walter, asked me what I thought about outlawing the Communist party, and I answered that it sometimes seemed to me the best way of handling the problem. So it sometimes does: if people are to be punished simply for belonging to the Communist party, which is happening all the time, it is only logical that membership should be proscribed by law. On the other hand, as I point out in the next chapter, it would be next to impossible to draft a law that would really work. Therefore, though I approve in theory of outlawing the party, I am opposed to it on practical grounds.

In the stress of this public hearing, with questions coming at me from all sides, I expressed myself badly, but Representative Kearney understood my uncertainty, for he said, "No matter which way it was done, somebody would be bound to be hurt?" Pleased that he had gone so directly to the heart of the dilemma, I replied, "Somebody will be hurt. There's no getting around it. I mean, innocent people will be hurt."

To me that is obvious. You can't fight Communism without hurting people, and you can't expect to devise a method that will hurt only the people who deserve to be hurt. The practical problem is to find a method that will do what has to be done while giving the innocent the maximum of protection.

This is so obvious to me that I was astonished when Whittaker Chambers, writing in *Life*, quoted my statement to the committee in order to express his disagreement. It is true that Chambers was speaking specifically of the two Congressional investigations into education, whereas I had in mind the whole campaign against the Communists, but I cannot share his conviction that no innocent person has been harmed by these particular investigations, and if one looks at the whole operation, including the McCarthy committee and all the various state committees, the evidence is overwhelming. I agree with Mr. Chambers that the damage is often exaggerated, not only by Communists and their sympathizers but also by overexcited liberals, but that is not the same thing as saying there is no damage.

In a manner of speaking, one of the chief purposes of the operation is to hurt people, as Mr. Chambers grants. Some one hundred educators, according to his statistics, have refused to tell one or the other of these two Congressional committees whether they are or have been Communists on the ground that to answer might incriminate them. Slightly more than half of these, he says, have been dismissed or suspended by the educational institutions employing them. The number dismissed has increased since he wrote the article, and in part, perhaps, because he wrote it.

Is there any likelihood that some of these people are innocent? I believe that any teacher who neglects his duties or abuses his privileges for the sake of advancing the interests of the Communist party deserves to be fired. As I have already indicated, it is conceivable to me that under some circumstances a Communist might be a conscientious and valuable teacher, and therefore I hold that each case ought to be judged on its merits; but, on the other hand, I am so certain that most Communists are incompetent teachers that I doubt whether in practice much damage is done by the firing of those who have been clearly identified as party members.

However, although all Communists invoke the protection of the Fifth Amendment, not all those who claim immunity are Communists. Suppose, for instance, that a witness has said, either in error or through malice, that you were once a member of the Communist party. If you deny the charge, it will be your word against the witness's, and, things being what they are, the committee is likely to take his word rather than yours. Thereupon you may find yourself indicted for perjury. You were never a Communist, but, because of the secrecy with which the party operates, that is a hard thing to prove. Moreover, a perjury trial, even if it ended by clearing you, would be an expensive and painful affair. You take your problem to a lawyer, and he tells you that you will save yourself trouble in the long run if you plead the Fifth Amendment.

There are other reasons for claiming immunity: some ex-Communists are unwilling to name friends who are or have been party members; some non-Communists disapprove of the investigations so strongly that they refuse to cooperate with them. It does not matter whether these are good reasons or bad; the important fact is that the Fifth Amendment may be invoked by people who are not members of the Communist party. I believe, therefore, that the claiming of immunity is not in itself valid reason for dismissal, and certain college administrations, to Mr. Chambers' obvious dismay, have taken that stand. Other colleges, however, have dismissed without any kind of hearing those teachers who refused to testify, and I am by no means satisfied that justice has always and invariably been done.

Nor am I as satisfied as Mr. Chambers is that the fifty-odd educators who admitted that they had once been Communists have got off scot-free. At the very least they have suffered some inconvenience, some stress and strain, some embarrassment. Perhaps, as Mr. Chambers would insist, anybody who was ever connected with the Communist party in any way deserves to suffer, but the fact remains that people have been hurt. Even if none of these men has lost his job, they must all be worried about their careers, and with some reason, for, as I can testify from personal experience, a known ex-Communist, even though he left the party years ago and has a long record of anti-Communist activity, is discriminated against in a variety of ways.

What happened as a result of my testimony before the Velde committee? Of the men I named as having been members of the Communist branch at Harvard in 1938–39, eight were subpoenaed by the committee. Four testified, and four claimed immunity. Two of the latter had left academic life. One of the others lost his job, and one didn't—Wendell Furry, who satisfied an investigating committee at Harvard that he had quit the party in 1947. Of the three who testified publicly that they had been party members, none, so far as I know, has been subject to disciplinary action, though all of them have doubtless suffered the kind of inconvenience I have mentioned.

In short, it appears that little damage was done, and I am happy that this is so. On the other hand, as I have already said, I cannot see that Communism was appreciably weakened by this particular inquiry. No conspiracy was exposed; no spies or saboteurs were apprehended. No record of current Communist activity of any sort was brought to light. Even as a piece of historical research, a study of Communism at Harvard fifteen years ago, the investigation produced no impressive results.

And I know of one innocent person, or at any rate a person of whose innocence I have no doubt, who was hurt by me, and might have been badly hurt. In naming men as Communists, I was careful to name only those whom I had actually seen at party meetings, but in a different connection, when I was off my guard, I alluded to a certain individual as if I knew that he had been a Communist. I did think he had been, but I should have pointed out that that was not knowledge but inference, and, as it turned out, a not very logical inference. Subsequently subpoenaed by the committee, this man hired counsel, had photostats made of articles he had written, and went to Washington for a private hearing. His evidence apparently convinced the committee's investigators, but my slip —my inexcusable failure to distinguish between a fact and an assumption—had cost him time, money, and worry. If he had lost his head, as he might have done, or if he had not been able to produce rather impressive evidence, or if the investigators had been less reasonable, his career might have been blasted.

Mr. Chambers himself has admitted that, as he looks back on the distant past, it becomes difficult to distinguish between first-hand knowledge and hearsay. When I was first summoned by the House Committee and began searching my memory, I realized with a shock that, of the scores of persons whom I had regarded as Communists in the thirties, there were relatively few whom I could positively identify as party members. And in spite of this realization, I committed, as I have told, an unpardonable blunder. This experience makes me skeptical when such a person as Louis Budenz produces long lists of names of persons who, he says, were known to him as Communists. When one thinks of the hundreds of witnesses who have appeared before the various investigating committees, the chance of error seems pretty large. And though it is generally true, as Chambers says, that the committee investigators examine the evidence with care, they would have to be superhuman not to make mistakes.

There have, moreover, been instances of deliberate misrepresentation. When I was in Seattle in the summer of 1948, I was told that one of the men the Canwell committee was determined to get was Professor Melvin Rader. Whether or not that was true, the committee did import an ex-Communist named George Hewitt, who testified that in either the summer of 1938 or the summer of 1939 Dr. Rader had been one of seventy educators attending a Communist party school in New York State. The only way Rader could disprove the charge was to account for all his time during two summers a decade earlier. By means of university records and other documents, he was able to show that during the whole of one summer and most of the other he hadn't been near New York, but there was an hiatus in the evidence, brief but long enough to make Hewitt's charges a possibility. Rader said that during this period he had been vacationing in the mountains, and finally a diligent newspaperman found proof for this claim and won a Pulitzer Prize with the stories he wrote about it. Hewitt was indicted for perjury, but somehow he managed to escape extradition and was never tried.

Even if the Velde committee and the Jenner committee are as scrupulous as Chambers supposes, they are only a few of the bodies that are engaged in investigating Communism. One of the oldest and most active of the state committees is the California Senate Committee on Un-American Activities, some of whose members I encountered at the Seattle Athletic Club in 1948. On March 19, 1953, Richard E. Combs, chief counsel for this committee, testified on its operations before the Jenner committee, calmly setting forth the blood-curdling details of what can only be described as a legislative conspiracy against academic freedom.

Mr. Combs stated that in March 1952 the committee called a meeting of the presidents of the colleges and universities in the southern part of California, and that a similar meeting was held in the northern part the following June. "A week thereafter," Mr. Combs continued, "eleven colleges joined in a cooperative plan to combat Communist infiltration." Robert Morris, counsel for the Senate subcommittee, asked, "Have you had any results since that time, since you have had this general alliance?"

Mr. Combs. About 100 faculty members have been removed from the faculties as a result of this plan since the 24th of last June.
Mr. Morris. So your testimony, Mr. Combs, is that since last June

—June 1952—because of the cooperative effort on the part of your committee and the various college presidents and their staffs, more than 100 members of California faculties have been removed from their teaching jobs?

Mr. Combs. That is correct. In addition to that, Mr. Morris, the committee deemed it expedient to indicate to the university administrators the necessity, particularly in the larger institutions, of employing full-time people who had had a practical experience in the field of counter-Communist activities, ex-FBI agents and ex-Navy and military intelligence men. That has been followed.

On the major colleges and campuses in California such persons are working and have been for almost since last June. They maintain a liaison with our committee. We in turn make available to them the accumulated documentation, the material that we have accumulated during the 14 years. But we soon found that it was even more necessary to prevent people from getting on faculties and obtaining positions in the educational institutions than it was to get rid of them once their positions became solidified.

So the committee developed a procedure whereby applicants for positions are referred to us, their names are, and if we do have any documentation concerning their Communist activity over a long period of time, we make that available to the university as a guide to indicate whether or not the individual should be employed.

The California committee, then, according to Mr. Combs's boasts, has done three things: it has got rid of more than one hundred teachers, it has established in the larger universities a system of special agents, and it has set up a blacklist. Senator Johnson, a member of the Jenner committee, made inquiry as to the methods by which suspect teachers were ousted. Mr. Combs explained:

The documentation on the individual, Senator, is given to the man on the campus whose full-time job it is to handle that type of matter as a liaison between the university and our committee. We meet with him if he believes that the man should be discharged, and we discuss the case. We analyze the type of front organization or organizations he belonged to, and the degree of activity that he took in it, the type of his associates, his activities in undercover meetings, and things of that type. We scrutinize the course to see whether he has reoriented it, to see if he made a medium of it for the dissemination of Communist propaganda.

All of these things are taken into consideration. Then when we are in agreement on the fact that he should be discharged, that information is given to the president of the institution. He then calls the individual before him and confronts him with the documentation, and in all of the 100 plus, I don't remember the exact number, but I do know there are more than 100, in no one of them has any individual refused to resign.

If he does refuse to resign, then the committee exercises its power of subpoena, places him under oath first in a closed hearing and then in an open hearing, but we have not had to do that since last June.

Not one of the one hundred plus has refused to resign! Does that prove that they were all card-carrying members of the Communist party? Not at all. Suppose you had belonged to a couple of party fronts five, ten, or fifteen years ago. Would you want to take a chance on a public hearing before a committee that had already judged you and found you guilty? Wouldn't you prefer to resign quietly? Not only Communists but ex-Communists and a variety of sympathizers and ex-sympathizers would be helpless against such methods. It would be hard to imagine a system of combating Communism that provided less protection for the innocent.

Mr. Combs was asked about Marxian propaganda in the classroom, and he admitted that he could remember only one or two examples. Communist teachers, he hastened to point out, did most harm by using classroom contacts to recruit students in Communist youth organizations. Pressed on the problem of propaganda, he gave an example from a class in public speaking:

Along came the next professor, and the name of the course was changed from public speaking to speech, and the only author they studied was John Stuart Mill, the Scotch philosopher. The one essay on which emphasis was placed was civil liberties. The professor concentrated his attention on freedom of speech rather than a flexible vocabulary and cited as an example of what was being done in the United States to deprive people of their right of free speech, and he cited the 13 members of the Communist Party of the United States, who according to him were deprived of their freedom of speech in the trial before Judge Medina at Foley Square.

If the man behaved in the fashion described, he obviously deserved to be fired for incompetence, even if the committee hadn't found "photostatic evidence of his affiliation with the Communist Party." But if the case were to be judged solely on the basis of Mr. Combs's account of the man's classroom activities, I should want to reserve judgment. I remember that I once got into difficulties because I assigned to my students a selection from Henry George's *Progress and Poverty* and challenged them to find the fallacy in his argument. Suppose a teacher assigned Mill's "On Liberty," not as the only text but as a major text, and asked his students to decide for themselves whether the trial of the Communist leaders violated the principles laid down by Mill. Couldn't this easily be misrepresented by a student with a grudge or a student who had been impressed—as what California student could fail to be —with the dangers of infiltration? And if this teacher had happened to belong to the League for Peace and Democracy or some other party front back in the thirties, what chance would he have?

I realize that I am dealing with hypothetical cases, but how else can one indicate the dangers that are inherent in the situation? The California system of combating Communism in education, as expounded by Mr. Combs, has such tremendous possibilities for evil that we cannot wait for some person as fortunate and as courageous as Melvin Rader was in the State of Washington to provide a concrete example of the harm it is doing. Look, for instance, at the appointment of special agents, a method endorsed by the Jenner committee in its summary report of July 17, 1953. Mr. Combs described the agents in these terms:

Well, at one large university in California the man who has been functioning since July is a former commander of Naval Intelligence. He is also a lawyer and has had 10 years experience combating Communism. He works full time.

At another large institution we have a man who is a graduate of the Federal Bureau of Investigation's academy, a graduate of Oxford University in England, who has had 17 years of police work and is a specialist in anti-Communist activity.

At a third large university we have another man who had experience in Naval Intelligence, was a commander, and his job was screening Communists in Germany after the war.

These are the types of men that the universities have employed, following our recommendation and who devote their full time to combating this infiltration, working with us.

The notion that a full-time expert is necessary to combat Communism in each university has the true California flavor. Even in a university with an outsize faculty such an expert ought to be able to make an exhaustive study into the private life of each teacher, and he would be only human if he sought to unearth as much subversion as possible. As I have suggested earlier, most teachers tend to be timid under any circumstances, and to the average teacher the knowledge that he was being subjected to scrutiny of that sort would be nearly paralyzing. And there would be some reason for caution, since unconventionality of any kind could be so easily mistaken for subversion. Education is bound to suffer, and it would be a miracle if there were not victims among teachers who were not only innocent of subversion but rather more able than the general run.

Mr. Combs also revealed that the committee relies on amateur as well as professional Red-hunters. "We get a great deal of voluntary assistance," he stated. "We couldn't possibly function without it. We didn't have any at first, but over the years we have a great many people who are in fairly good circumstances and who do this without pay at all, investigative work, reporting, etc." Applied to the colleges, this means that teachers are not only being watched by full-time official agents but are also constantly under surveillance by colleagues, students, or outsiders.

The blacklist appears to be extensive:

Senator Johnson. I believe you brought out that there were 100 teachers that have been discharged?
Mr. Combs. Yes, sir.

Senator Johnson. You do not know how many hundreds you kept from getting jobs because of their connections with the Communist party, do you?

Mr. Combs. I can only give an estimate; at least that many if not more.

Senator Johnson. You have found out that it is better to get them out before they get in?

Mr. Combs. Very definitely.

Senator Johnson. In other words, an ounce of prevention is better than a pound of cure?

Mr. Combs. We feel very strongly that that is the case. We don't feel that that means we should neglect removing them, but then you run into academic freedom and tenure, front committees organized to protect their rights, Communist recruiters who try to paint them as martyrs, raising of funds, and all that sort of thing.

Mr. Morris asked Mr. Combs: "Suppose that you are doing this preventive work, namely, preventing the Communists from coming on the faculty. Suppose that you have a professor coming from the north or south or east of the country, what steps do you take in order to find out about this man's background?" Mr. Combs promptly replied that one of the things he did was to get in touch with the investigative staff of the Jenner committee. Assuming that he finds the investigative staff of the Velde committee equally cooperative, I wonder what would happen to the victim of my mistake if he should try to get a teaching job in California. Even if the records showed that he had produced evidence to prove that he had never been a Communist and that I had written a letter correcting the implications of my testimony, would a special agent be convinced and would a college administrator dare to take a chance?

Nothing could be more indicative of the American state of mind than the fact that almost no attention was paid to these nightmarish revelations.[1] The Jenner committee, indeed, in its summary report, found the California plan so admirable that it recommended it to the legislators and educators of other states. To the Senators it seems neither absurd nor dangerous for a so-called "fact-finding" committee to have established a network of spies on the campuses of California. Nor is this surprising, for all the legislative committees have arrogated to themselves more and more power. And this is inevitably power to hurt people.

The McCarthy committee has produced the clearest record of damage done, and this record is the best indication of the dangers inherent in the powers given to or usurped by legislative investigations. So far as McCarthy is concerned, we do not have to speculate as to whether he has hurt innocent people; we know that he has, though we shall probably never know just how many. He has blackened the reputations of General Marshall, Charles Bohlen, Allen Dulles, James Wechsler, Nathan Pusey, and countless others. He has not only crippled the Voice of America, as already noted, but has deprived such able men as Theodore Kaghan and Reed Harris

[1] So little attention has been paid that it still remains a possibility that the revelations were in fact a nightmare. California educators have denied that any such conferences as Mr. Combs described ever took place, that special agents have been appointed, that any large number of teachers were dismissed. On the other hand, Hugh M. Burns, chairman of the California committee, has written me: "The colleges have named liaison officers to work with us in exchanging information and are not necessarily full-time investigating agents. They are people who, in the main, have had some experience in this field and can therefore evaluate the records of suspected subversive individuals." Even, however, if it turns out that Mr. Combs was indulging in a private fantasy it is a fantasy that, if the Jenner committee has its way, will soon become a reality.

of their jobs. He has brought about the banning of books, defended a sweeping attack on the Protestant clergy, and called into question the loyalty of scores of Americans whose only crime was the fact that they had criticized Joseph McCarthy.

What is so spectacularly true of the McCarthy investigation is in some measure true of all the other investigations, state and federal, that are going on. There is room for argument as to how effective they are, just as there is room for argument as to how much harm they do, but there is not much room for argument when one tries to strike a balance. They would have to be either a great deal more effective or a great deal less harmful to justify their existence.

Says Mr. Chambers, "The one instantly verifiable fact of the witch-hunt is this: of more than 50 people questioned before Congressional committees in the last five years about active participation in a secret Communist conspiracy within the United States Government (often including espionage), only two have ever been prosecuted." This fact, which, by some strange twist of logic, he interprets as a tribute to the investigating committees, seems to me, on the contrary, a striking demonstration of their ineffectiveness. Whatever other damage Communists may do, their greatest threat lies in espionage, and against espionage legislative investigation proves to be no weapon at all.

I think Mr. Chambers must have realized that he had failed to make a case for the committees, for, at the end of his article, after quoting what I had said about innocent people getting hurt, he shifted his ground in an interesting fashion. "Those thousands of Americans," he wrote, "who watch their TV screens . . . may see what Mr. Hicks sees, but many of them

also see something else. They see not only the plight of the
witnesses. They also see the purpose of the congressmen and
senators whom they have elected, in part to pursue such investigations. And while they too may be aware that in any
fight innocent people may always be hurt, they also know that
in the fight against Communism not all the people being hurt
are witnesses before congressional committees."

Mr. Chambers went on to speak of a friend of his who had a
son who was a jet pilot in Korea. People like this friend, he
said, feel "that there is a connection between the war in Korea
and the war against Communism at home. They sense, too,
perhaps without being able or willing to spell it out for themselves, or you, that if Communism succeeds in winning that
larger war, of which both of these inseparable wars are part,
all freedom will have become academic, merely academic."

But we who worry about the plight of witnesses, or some of
us at any rate, also realize that the war in Korea and the war
against Communism at home are inseparable, and that life
will be unbearable if the war against Communism is lost. We
have no disagreement with Whittaker Chambers or his friend
Sherman Flanagan on those grounds. We simply ask questions about the way in which the war against Communism at
home is being conducted.

On the day on which I read Chambers' article I received a
letter from a friend whose son had just been drafted. "I suppose," she wrote, "that you have often wondered how you
would face such a thing as your son going off to kill or be
killed, if you had a son. I have always felt it could not be faced.
I'm no India Edwards. If he gets hurt it's because I didn't
know how to help it, not because I want the world made safe

for democracy. Personally, I want the world made safe for my sons."

This, I submit, is an understandable way for a parent to feel, but I wouldn't regard a woman—or a man—in that frame of mind as the best possible judge of foreign policy. Nor am I sure that a man with a son in Korea would be likely to make the wisest decision on how the fight against Communism at home ought to be conducted. If Mr. Chambers hadn't had an uncomfortable feeling that maybe innocent people are being hurt, I don't believe that he would have found it necessary to make his appeal to emotions that are perfectly human but not always trustworthy.

X

How to Fight Communism

If, as I have been arguing, legislative investigations do more harm than good, that does not mean that we can disregard the danger of Communism. It is important, with all the current confusion, to know what not to do, but it is more important to know what must be done.

One of my principal objections to the antics of Senator Mc-Carthy and to the activities of legislative investigations in general is the fact that they give people the impression that something really important is being done, whereas actually, even if their most extravagant claims were justified, their work would have only minor significance. If every Russian agent in America were caught tomorrow, all the big problems of winning the war would remain. For the big problems are military and diplomatic.

No one wants another world war, fought with atom bombs and other incalculably destructive weapons, but readiness for such a war is the condition of survival itself. Where Communist aggression has been checked, it has been checked by force. It was in 1946 and 1947, when our armies had been demobilized and our factories converted to peacetime production, that Russian Communism pushed its borders westward, and it may be, as Winston Churchill has said, that only fear of the atom bomb kept it from sweeping across the continent of Europe. We learned our lesson and undertook the building of a gigantic military machine and the arming of our allies as well as ourselves. We have already had to fight in Korea, and we don't know where we may have to fight tomorrow. We Americans don't like to see our sons in uniform, and we don't like to pay large taxes to maintain a military machine in what is ostensibly a time of peace, but these are things that we have to do.

Most of us realize equally well, though there is plenty of quibbling about details, that we must fight Communism by helping the non-Communist countries. It is not merely a matter of strengthening them, so that they can fight if necessary; Communism does not thrive in countries that are prospering. The problem of winning and holding allies, as our statesmen have been discovering, is infinitely difficult, but we do have our tremendous productive power to help us. In the wise use of that power lies the best hope of preventing World War III, as well as of winning it if it comes.

These are the fundamentals, and we must always bear them in mind. The fight against Communism in America is only part of our job—an important part, of course, but a very small part.

In deciding how to protect ourselves against the American Communists, we must begin by asking what they can do to hurt us. So far as anyone knows, the American Communists have been most harmful when they have served as spies. To cope with espionage, we need specially trained men, professionals, and in the FBI and the other intelligence agencies of the government we have full-time spy-hunters. Much of the work of these agencies is necessarily carried on in secret, and therefore it is hard to know how effective they are. Certainly they are not perfectly successful. General Bedell Smith, while he was chief of Military Intelligence, said that in all probability every government agency, including his own, was infiltrated by Russian spies. Nevertheless, the cases that do get into the papers make it clear that the FBI and the other groups of the same sort are doing an effective job.

Because so much depends on the FBI, the rest of us must support its agents in any way we can, and those of us who, as ex-Communists, may have information of value, ought to make it available. I have seen a good deal of FBI agents at one time or another, and sometimes I have been impatient with the methods they use. (I once asked an agent why, instead of coming to see me in a certain matter, he hadn't gone to the library and looked through a file of the *New Masses*. "Never thought of it," he answered cheerfully. "You see, you have a literary mind, and I have a detective mind.") By and large, however, I have found that these men are well-informed and scrupulous. They are looking for evidence, and they seem as pleased with evidence of innocence as with evidence of guilt.

The work of the FBI is quiet, and it seems slow, and many people have wondered whether there wasn't some other, quicker way of dealing with the Communist problem. The Smith Act and the Internal Security Act of 1950 both aim at that end, and for a long time there has been talk about a law making the Communist party illegal. Each of these measures ought to be examined.

The Smith Act, under which several dozen leaders of the Communist party have been or are being tried, forbids the advocacy of the overthrow of the government by force and violence. It has been criticized by many non-Communists on the ground that it abrogates the right of freedom of speech, since it is directed not against what people do but what they say. It has always been recognized, however, that the right of free speech is not unlimited, and most liberals have accepted Justice Holmes' principle that speech may be restricted when there is "a clear and present danger" that it may bring about an evil of a sort Congress has a right to legislate against. In deciding on the constitutionality of the Smith Act, the majority of the Supreme Court maintained that there was such a danger, while the minority denied it.

Now it is hard to see that Communist teachings are likely to result in a revolutionary uprising—which is what is suggested by "the overthrow of the government by force and violence." In a real sense, as we have seen, that is not even what they are aimed at. What the Communists are working for, by word and deed, is the defeat of the United States at the hands of a foreign power, and that is the crime with which they should be charged.

The Internal Security Act, then, seems a more effective weapon than the Smith Act, for it attacks the Communists as foreign agents. Like the Smith Act, however, it has been slow in its operations. When the top leaders of the Communist party were tried in New York under the Smith Act, the trial went on for month after month, and even when they had been convicted there was a time-consuming appeal to the Supreme Court. The Internal Security Act established a Subversive Activities Control Board, which held hearings for more than a year before coming to the conclusion that the party was "a foreign-dominated revolutionary movement." As a result of this decision, the party was required to submit annually to the Department of Justice a financial statement and a list of officers and members. The party, of course, began to fight the measure in the courts, and the legal struggle dragged on. There would, one could foresee, be further evasions if the constitutionality of the act were upheld.

Many persons have felt that it would be quicker as well as more honest to outlaw the party. The problem, however, is how to formulate a law that gets the Communists and only the Communists. If a law is passed outlawing the party by name, the name will, of course, be changed. If it outlaws any party that engages in such-and-such activities, there is always a danger that it may be used against unpopular organizations that have no connection with Communism.

The truth is that we don't need any new laws. As many observers have pointed out, the American people have a wonderful faith in legislation, and we have adopted innumerable laws, federal and state, designed to protect us against Communism. One of the most popular devices is also one of the most futile—the loyalty oath, which never gives a Communist a moment's pause but may embarrass some honest and useful dissenter or eccentric. Certain sections of the McCarran-Walter Act of 1952, aimed at protecting this country against foreign subversives, manage to bar not only persons who couldn't possibly do us any harm but also persons who might do us a lot of good. The more anti-Communist legislation we get, the greater the danger that innocent persons will be hurt, with no compensating gain in security.

There are on the statute books adequate laws against

espionage, sabotage, and such other overt acts as Communists may commit against the security of the United States. The problem is one of enforcement—primarily of detection—and it is a problem that can be handled only by professionals. It is true now, and it has always been true, that Communists who do anything against the government can be punished— if they can be caught. If our intelligence agencies are incompetent, new legislation will not help matters in the least. If, as I believe, they are reasonably efficient, we are worrying unnecessarily. As General Smith admitted, no intelligence agency is successful all the time, but that does not mean that we are at the mercy of the Communists.

But, some people will protest, even if we do have all the laws we need to protect us against Communist deeds, what about Communist propaganda? What about it, indeed? It can be dangerous, make no mistake about that, but can the danger be combated by the passing of laws? Should we, for instance, forbid the teaching of Marxism and, as has been suggested, remove all Marxist books from our libraries? The very notion is ridiculous. Marxism is part of our intellectual heritage, and no law can eradicate it. If we were to eliminate all the books that have been influenced by Marxism, to say nothing of those that expound Marxist ideas in order to quarrel with them, there would be great gaps on the library shelves, and we should be vastly poorer. Furthermore, if I may play a little longer with this preposterous suggestion, we should be depriving ourselves of one key to the understanding of our opponents, who always talk and sometimes act like Marxists. And we should gain absolutely nothing, for the Communists would know how to disguise their propaganda so that the law couldn't touch it.

Should we, then, simply deny Communists the right to write and speak? Again we would make ourselves ridiculous. A couple of years ago the student body of Wesleyan University in Connecticut planned a conference on Communism. The idea was: this is what we're fighting; let's try to understand it. After lining up a number of anti-Communist authorities, the committee in charge said to themselves, "Look here, if we want to know what Communism is, the thing to do is to invite a couple of Communists to speak to the conference." So they asked Henry Winston and John Gates, high officials of the party, who accepted. And then the top blew off: patriotic organizations in the vicinity made such a noise that the invitations were withdrawn.

What would have happened if Winston and Gates had gone to Wesleyan? They would, necessarily, have expounded the current party line: South Korea invaded North Korea; UN intervention was simple Wall Street imperialism; the Soviet Union was the bulwark of world peace. And they would have found no takers. But even if they had managed to set forth Communist doctrine in some persuasive form, there were still a dozen anti-Communist speakers to expose and refute them, to say nothing of all the opportunities of the faculty in their regular classes. As it was, the students couldn't understand why the people of Middletown were so frightened, and some of them may have got the idea that the whole fight against Communism was a little phony.

Actually, the indignant citizens of Middletown weren't

worrying about whether the ideas of Winston and Gates would be refuted or not. If you had pinned them down, they would have admitted that they didn't expect the two Communists to make any converts. What they were doing was expressing their anger against Communism, and that is perfectly comprehensible. The pity is that they didn't find some less dangerous way of giving vent to their emotions.

I see no reason why we should be frightened by Communist teachings so long as they are labeled as such. In the thirties, when the atmosphere was so much more favorable to Communism than it is at present, I spoke as an avowed Communist at Wesleyan and many other colleges, all of which are still standing. If today we cannot meet the arguments of an avowed Communist, there is something wrong with us. I am not recommending indifference to Communist propaganda. I don't think we can sit back and say, "Oh, pooh, nobody will be taken in by that." But I do think we can deal with Communism when it is in the open.

What complicates the problem is the fact that so much Communist propaganda is falsely labeled. Back in the militant days before the Popular Front, Communists did not conceal the fact that they proposed to make a revolution in America on the Russian model. (Even then, of course, they concealed the extent to which they were controlled by Russia.) William Z. Foster, the party's candidate for President in 1932, the one I and fifty-one other intellectuals endorsed, set forth his platform in a book that was frankly called *Toward Soviet America.* "To escape the encroaching capitalist starvation," he wrote, "and to emancipate themselves, the workers of the world, including those in this country, must and will take the revolutionary way out of the crisis. That is, they will carry out a militant policy now in defense of their daily interests and, finally, following the example of the Russian workers, they will abolish capitalism and establish Socialism." Since "the capitalists will never voluntarily give up control of society and abdicate their system of exploiting the masses," the revolution, he insisted, can only be won by force. When it is won, the dictatorship of the proletariat will be established, with "the Communist party functioning alone as the party of the toiling masses."

This, if not wholly frank, was frank enough. In the Popular Front period, however, all talk of violent revolution and the dictatorship of the proletariat ceased. Communism was now represented as "Twentieth-Century Americanism," and all Communists insisted that they were the staunchest defenders of democracy. The Popular Front became officially the Democratic Front, with the slogan, "For jobs, security, democracy, and peace." The party issued a pamphlet containing the Constitution of the United States and the Declaration of Independence, with an introduction by Earl Browder. "Few countries," Mr. Browder said, "have a richer heritage of traditions of revolutionary struggles for human freedom than the United States. We Communists," he continued, "know we belong in the camp of democracy and progress, as the most conscious and loyal fighters and organizers of the fight against reaction and fascism. *We of the Communist Party,*" he insisted in italics, "*never did and never will hold to a program of forcible establishment of socialism against the will of the people.*" On February 12, 1936, Browder delivered an address in Springfield, Illinois, in which he argued that if Lin-

coln were alive he would be a Communist—or would, at any
rate, be glad to work with the Communists in the Democratic
Front. When Browder sought to defend the Moscow purges,
he did a little research, came up with the names of Benedict
Arnold and Aaron Burr, and published a pamphlet entitled, "Traitors in American History: Lessons of the Moscow
Trials."

The new line was a boon to the concealed Communists and
the fellow travelers, for they were able to represent themselves
as liberals and progressives. This, as we know, was the great
period of Communist infiltration into government and labor
and of Communist influence in cultural matters. In this period
many persons who were *not* interested in the expansion of
Russian Communism joined the Communist party because
they were interested in fighting fascism. Many others
knowingly cooperated with the Communists because they
belived that the Communists were working for the same
goals as they were. And still others unknowingly supported
party fronts because they were unable to tell the difference
between real liberals and the Communist imitation.

Although the party line has changed several times since
then, it has never returned to the candid militancy of the
twenties and early thirties. Whatever the party is up to, it
always pretends to be nobly serving some great liberal idea.
This was a little difficult to manage in the 1939–41 period,
but there was some honest isolationist and pacifist sentiment
behind which the party line could hide. After the invasion of
Russia, of course, the Communists were again anti-fascists,
friends of democracy, and the most ardent of patriots.

Since the war, the party has again been clamoring for peace, but with so much emphasis on Russian benevolence and American warmongering that the straight party line is repugnant to most Americans. The concealed Communists and fellow travelers, however, have found ways in which the line can be gently but satisfactorily modified. Only an out-and-out Communist insisted that South Korea had invaded North Korea, but a secret Communist could point out that each government had been intriguing against the other and that therefore it made little difference which invaded which, and add that the South Korean government of Syngman Rhee was notoriously corrupt. The party spokesman demanded that the United Nations accept the North Korean terms for a truce; the sympathizer (or secret Communist) observed judiciously that a case could be made for the return of all prisoners. When anti-Semitism flared up in Russia and the satellites in the winter of 1952–53, the spokesman proclaimed that Slansky and the other Czech Jews, the Jewish doctors in Moscow, Ana Pauker, and all the rest were guilty as charged, and that the Zionists were plotting to overthrow the Soviet Union. The sympathizer carried on a diversionary action by asking whether anti-Semitism wasn't responsible for the death sentences given Julius and Ethel Rosenberg.

I am not saying that everybody who thinks we can have a negotiated peace with Russia, everybody who believes our intervention in Korea was a mistake, everybody who has doubts about the execution of the Rosenbergs, is a Communist or a fellow traveler. Our whole dilemma arises from the fact that that isn't true. The views set forth by the camouflaged Communists are also held by a certain number of people who would continue to hold them, as of course no Communist would, if the party line changed. The truth is that the Communists, through their technique of camouflage, have not only had some success in concealing their own operations; they have managed to introduce a demoralizing confusion into the liberal camp.

Later on I have more to say about that confusion, its causes and consequences, but let us look at it for the moment simply as it bears on the problem of Communist propaganda. To begin with, there is the party line, which is by no means an honest statement of the party's aims, but is at the moment so emphatically pro-Russian and anti-American that few people are likely to fall for it. The secret Communists and close fellow travelers, as we have seen, take a position that supports the line but cannot be labeled Communist. The more remote fellow traveler may express disagreement with the line on this point or that, though he always comes back to the fact that Russia must be given the benefit of every doubt. Then there is the befuddled liberal, who does not want to help Russia or the Communists but happens to be taken in by some of the specious arguments of the sympathizers. And finally there are the persons who have arrived quite independently at similar conclusions.

I believe that propaganda can never be dealt with by law, and that any attempt so to deal with it is dangerous. But whether I am right or wrong, the futility of trying to deal with Communist propaganda by law ought to be obvious. There would be no point in a law aimed merely at suppressing propaganda that was labeled as Communist, for this does little or no harm in the present situation. And if a law sought to stamp out the subtle propaganda that may have some effect, it would curb the freedom of speech of a large number of loyal Americans.

Clearly this is a job that can only be done by patient, well-informed analysis. It has to be done by persons who are not heresy-hunters but who are not afraid of being called Red-baiters and witch-burners by the Communists, crypto-Communists, and confused liberals. It is a job that today, for reasons I discuss in the following chapters, is not being done as well as it ought to be. But that does not mean that there is any different or easier or quicker way of doing it.

There, then, is a program. It points out that the great task, the task that dwarfs all others, is military and diplomatic. It suggests that Communist espionage and sabotage can be taken care of by the FBI and that we don't need legislative inquiries or special laws against subversion. It recommends that Communist propaganda should be met as other propaganda is met, by reliance on truth and reason. If it recognizes that Communist Russia is strong, it insists that the United States isn't weak. It is not sensational enough to make newspaper headlines, but that might be in its favor.

XI

The Liberals Who Haven't Learned

Whatever may have been true in the past, the very great majority of American intellectuals today are anti-Communist. Some of us had to learn the hard way, but we learned. This being true, it would seem that we ought to have no trouble at all in disposing of Communism on the intellectual front, but actually, as everybody knows, this is a period of the most abysmal confusion. Self-seeking politicians make all they can of the confusion, but they are not solely responsible for it. It is to a considerable extent a dish that some of the intellectuals have cooked for themselves. In particular, two groups of intellectuals, both comparatively small, have blurred and distorted the issues of the present struggle. On the one hand, a prejudice in favor of the Soviet Union persists in the thinking of a few, some of whom say, and quite possibly believe, that they are opposed to Communism. On the other hand, certain intellectuals have reacted so violently against Communism, frequently as a result of their past association with it, that they have completely lost their bearings.

The intellectuals with a pro-Soviet bias describe themselves as liberals, and they are likely to boast of their open minds. Their favorite word is "but." "North Korea was guilty of aggression, but . . ." "There is no civil liberty in Russia, but . . ." "We must protect our country against

Communism, but . . ." Some of the people who talk this way
are Communists and close sympathizers; they are the Fake Liberals. But there are others who really believe what they say.

This is the kind of distinction one cannot expect a Congressional committee to make, but it is a real distinction just the
same. There are people who are in no way subject to Communist discipline but nevertheless are incapable of recognizing
the Soviet Union for what it is. In order to deal with them, we
have to try to understand how they acquired this peculiar
twist.

As I pointed out in talking about the twenties, there was in
that decade a loose kind of united front against the *status quo*.
The intellectuals were almost unanimous in their distaste
for a business civilization and in their willingness to accept
as allies all enemies of the existing order. Russia, with all its
faults, was regarded as being on "our" side because it represented something new in the world and because it was hated
and feared by the proponents and beneficiaries of the *status
quo*. Lots of people felt that way in the twenties and again
in the later thirties, when the Soviet Union was believed to be
the bulwark of the anti-fascist cause, and again also in the early
forties, when Russia was our ally. And there are a few who
still do. They still believe that a liberal is one who opposes
the government and gives Russia the benefit of every doubt.
The world has changed, but they haven't. They are the Retarded Liberals.

Because a Fake Liberal does his best to sound like a Retarded Liberal, it is difficult to tell them apart except by
taking into account what they have done as well as what they
have said. If, for instance, a person has followed the party line

through a series of shifts, and if he has been trusted with responsibility in organizations dominated by the party, it is safe to conclude that he is a fellow traveler and therefore a Fake Liberal. Such a person is Corliss Lamont, son of the late Thomas Lamont of J. P. Morgan and Co.

Lamont was recently in the news when he defied Senator McCarthy. The Senator, currently investigating publications used by the Army, found a couple of Lamont's books on the list and subpoenaed their author, as he had subpoenaed various other authors who were supposed to have Communist sympathies. (Authors' names make news.) Not claiming immunity but simply refusing to testify on the ground that the committee had no right to question him with regard to his writings, Lamont invited citation for contempt. His stand, from my point of view, was both right and courageous, and if his challenge should result in a court test of the McCarthy committee's power, one could only regard him as a public benefactor.

But if I feel compelled to support Lamont in his battle with McCarthy, I cannot accept his description of himself as a "moderate, independent, and freewheeling American dissenter." In a statement he released to the press, he listed some fifty issues on which he had disagreed with the Communists, mostly "in my primary field of concentration, philosophy." He was, he said, a humanist rather than a dialectical materialist, and he opposed "current Communist dogmatism in science." He had even gone so far, he insisted, as to defend George Santayana when the Communists in the United States attacked him as a Fascist. But, so far as one could learn from the papers, his statement did not mention a single important

political issue on which his position has differed from that of
the Communist party, nor can I recall a disagreement of that
kind. In 1939 he defended the Nazi-Soviet nonaggression
pact. (When I was leaving the party, because of the pact, he
urged me not to "take this fateful turn at what has become
for a number of people a fundamental parting of the ways.")
During the wartime honeymoon he was chairman of the
National Council of American-Soviet Friendship. He was
one of the sponsors of the Cultural and Scientific Conference
for World Peace in 1949, and in 1952 he ran for the Senate
as candidate of the Progressive party.

It is true that Lamont has never felt obliged to agree with
every word that appears in the *Daily Worker,* but, in view of
his record, *The Independent Mind* seemed a singular title for
the collection of his essays, published in 1951. There was, to
be sure, an air of independence in a passage such as this:
"Although completely rejecting red-baiting, progressives
should have no hesitation in making honest criticisms of the
Communist party, as, for example, in regard to its limited conception of civil liberties, its ridiculous position that the Soviet
Union has already become the practically perfect state, and
its attempt to whitewash the North Koreans." But the leaders
of the Communist party have no reason to be worried about
Lamont, and they knew what they were doing when they
backed him for Senator. As one reads on, one learns that the
"independent mind" functions in this fashion:

The obvious truth is that Soviet Russia, like the United States,
Great Britain or Sweden, is a mixture of good and bad, of note-
worthy accomplishments and distressing failures and a sincere
striving for future betterment. . . . It seems to me that the way

to avoid the extremes I have been describing is to take a middle-of-the-road position which gives honest consideration to both the defects and virtues of Soviet Russia. For instance, it is plain that the Soviet Union lags lamentably behind the United States in the development of civil liberty and political democracy, notwithstanding grave American backslidings in those fields. At the same time the Soviet Russians have forged far ahead of America in the establishment of ethnic equality and racial democracy among the more than 150 different minor nationalities and races that live within the far-flung Soviet domain. It would be possible to make a number of other comparisons between American and Soviet life, some of them favorable to the USA, some of them favorable to the USSR.

This bland judiciousness, which had a more plausible air before the anti-Semitism of the winter of 1953 had exposed the character of Soviet "ethnic equality and racial democracy," paves the way for what Lamont has to say in his crucial essay, "The Myth of Soviet Aggression." Here he lists twenty reasons for believing that Russia has no aggressive intentions, and a prettier collection of half-truths and untruths you could not ask for. But what he does not say is even more significant than what he does. He ignores the absorption of the Baltic republics, the partition of Poland, and the war against Finland. He ignores the processes by which the satellites have been transformed into Russian colonies. He ignores the broken agreements, the hostile gestures, the bellicose speeches. As for Korea, "there is no evidence that Soviet Russia was responsible."

It remains for Mr. Lamont to describe "The Myth of 'The Free World,' " and then to dwell on the horrors of a third world war, and his job is done. It is a job that the *Daily Worker* couldn't do better, nor half so well. The book is obviously calculated to weaken the American will to resist Soviet aggression, and, in view of his record, I find it impossible to believe that Lamont didn't know what he was doing.

If Lamont gives us a first-rate example of Fake Liberalism, we can find what is almost certainly Retarded Liberalism, mixed with a certain amount of Fake Liberalism, in the files of the *Nation*. Look, for instance, at a special issue of that magazine, dated June 28, 1952, that was devoted to the subject of civil liberties in the United States. The question, as raised by Editor Freda Kirchwey, was, "How Free Is Free?" The answer was that freedom was in a bad way. Indeed, in her prefatory article Miss Kirchwey compared her little band of fighters for freedom to soldiers in a desperate and perhaps hopeless battle.

As Richard Rovere pointed out in the *New Leader*, the issue as a whole gave an impression that was essentially false. He quoted from an article by Ralph S. Brown, Jr., of Yale, who wrote: "Many people today refuse to admit that there is any difference between political liberalism and Communism, and assert the right and duty to impose on others their own standards of belief and conduct." Certainly there are such people, but, as Rovere pointed out, they have scarcely succeeded in suppressing political liberalism. The leaders of the administration, he said—this, of course, was before the election—were proud to call themselves liberals, and many Republicans insisted that they were liberals too. Senator McCarthy, he observed, had some enemies in high office, including the then President of the United States, Harry S. Truman.

One of the longest articles was "The Battle of the Books" by

Matthew Josephson. There was nothing to indicate that Josephson, who had been active in party fronts for twenty-odd years, might be a biased witness, nor did Josephson himself suggest in any way that he had a special interest—which would be a legitimate enough interest if openly stated—in the publication of left-wing books. His expressed concern was all for the "liberal" books that, according to him, either were being denied publication by timid publishers or were being banned by libraries or school boards. It is interesting to observe that a few months later one of the largest publishers in the country published a biography of Sidney Hillman by Mr. Josephson.

Some of the incidents described by Josephson in his article are indeed lamentable, and other lamentable incidents have taken place since the article appeared. No one can doubt that there are people in this country who enjoy burning books. Yet the careful reader will see that Josephson was determined to make a bad situation seem vastly worse than it was. Perhaps the clearest evidence is in a paragraph that is not exactly relevant to the author's thesis but helps to achieve the effect he is seeking. "How does the hysteria in 1919, after World War I," he asks, "compare with that of today?" After briefly describing that unhappy episode, he says, "Yet all this *furor Americanus* seems ill organized, spontaneous, and full of hearty animal spirits compared with the present movement." Even the sketchy account I have given of the Palmer Red raids will suggest that Mr. Josephson's memory is, in this instance, not to be relied on.

The special issue of the *Nation* contained articles arguing that McCarthyism was triumphant in the theater, the movies, the radio, and television. Kirtley Mather denounced "the campaign to paralyze all independent thought, discussion, and dissent concerning America's foreign policy." Arthur Eggleston asserted that "the witch hunt, which began with 'foreign agents,' is being extended to cover liberals of all shades of economic and political belief." Carey McWilliams maintained that the "witch hunt" was making matters worse for Negroes and Jews. (It will be remembered that 1952 was the first year in our history in which no Negro was lynched.) Several articles were required to show how bad conditions were in education. Mr. Rovere summed up the issue in this way: "This is a piece of work that depends for its effect on canny editing, and the effect it achieves is to encourage the world to accept Radio Moscow's view of the United States, the view of this society as a disintegrating democracy, one in which the hooligan element not only strives for power, as it does everywhere, but has already achieved it."

The acceptance of Radio Moscow's view of the United States is accompanied by a certain willingness to go along with Radio Moscow's view of Russia. That is not to say that the *Nation* is uncritical of the Soviet Union but merely that it is quite willing to hunt for excuses for whatever Russia does. As recently as 1950, in an issue celebrating its eighty-fifth anniversary, the *Nation* apologized for Soviet aggression. Since that time it has taken a somewhat harsher line, but even now its editors are quick to say anything that can be said in defense of the Soviet Union. They are still, one feels, longing to be convinced that it is not the ruthless, aggressive totalitarian dictatorship it so obviously is, but the great force for progress they once believed it to be.

But what difference does it make? Is anyone influenced by the *Nation?* I'm afraid so. When I wrote an article analyzing the bias of the eighty-fifth anniversary issue, the protests were numerous and full of pain and indignation. One of the bitterest came from a clergyman, the Reverend Henry A. Atkinson of the Church Peace Union. After some less than charitable remarks about my character and motives, Dr. Atkinson wrote: "I have known intimately for many years the people who are responsible for editing the *Nation.* Miss Kirchwey and Mr. del Vayo and their associates are honorable, intelligent, trustworthy, and above suspicion in thought and action." Therefore, the implication seems clear, Dr. Atkinson was willing to accept at face value anything the magazine might publish. Miss Kirchwey also wrote a reply to my article, in the course of which she quoted from various eminent persons who had written her enthusiastically about the special issue.

The pro-Soviet bias dies hard. After I broke with the Communist party, I was always coming across people who weren't Communists and never had been but who would say, "Don't you feel that Russia *had* to make the pact with Germany?" Such people welcomed our wartime alliance with Russia not merely because we needed all the allies we could get but also because they felt that there was some special virtue in being on the same side as the Soviet Union. After the war, when I was fuming against Soviet aggression in the Balkans, the Retarded Liberals would say, "But at least the masses are going to be better off."

It has grown harder and harder to maintain this faith, but it does survive. According to what Freda Kirchwey was saying just the other day, and may be saying again tomorrow, Russia is on the right side of the great revolution of our times and we are on the wrong side. Kingsley Martin, editor of the London *New Statesman and Nation,* who might be described as Miss Kirchwey's British counterpart, declared not so long ago that the Russians are a prosperous, happy, and peace-loving people. The Retarded Liberals have been giving Russia the benefit of every doubt for so long that the habit persists in spite of everything that has happened. That we may at any moment become involved in a shooting war with the Soviet Union is something they will not let themselves believe, and hence reasonable measures of protection are as abhorrent to them as unreasonable ones. The only villain on their horizon is Joe McCarthy, and they see him eight or ten times as big as life.

We forget sometimes about the ordinary rank-and-file liberals, but they can be found everywhere, and very good people they are—civic-minded, hard-working in thankless causes, the people you can count on. They take the unpopular side on local issues: work against the real-estate lobby to get public housing, fight racial discrimination, join committees to expose vice and corruption. Like most liberals everywhere, they tend to be a little self-righteous about their independence and intelligence, but they can be forgiven their foibles. They are not Communists; some of them have never seen a real live Communist or read an official Communist publication. And in the present state of affairs they are all for the United States and all against Russia.

And yet there is in some of them a streak of something like Retarded Liberalism. These minor-league liberals are so used to standing up for dissenters that they cannot or will not understand what they are up against when they tangle with the Communists. Certain small-city liberals find it almost impossible to believe that a well-educated, soft-voiced, properly dressed person, the kind of person they would be glad to entertain in their homes, can be, or can have been, a Communist; and if they are convinced on that score, they assume that he can't be, or have been, a "bad" Communist. Hence the persistent belief, so widespread among the ordinary liberals of the hinterlands, that Alger Hiss could not be guilty of the crimes with which Whittaker Chambers charged him.

Not long ago I was talking with four liberals, two lawyers and two professors, quite typical in their good works and their cautious disagreement with majority sentiment in their predominantly conservative community, but if anything more sophisticated than the average. We were talking about the testimony of a certain ex-Communist before a House committee, and one of the professors said, "Imagine it; he says that so-and-so and so-and-so and so-and-so are Communists." The other professor and the two lawyers responded with the skeptical and superior smiles that were expected of them. I pointed out that all three of the persons named had worked in party fronts for years. "That doesn't prove that they're Communists," I said, "but you certainly can't take it for granted that they aren't." The four of them looked unhappy and a little sore, but they realized that I was right. Finally one of the lawyers said, "Well, I can't stand informers."

Among some of the liberals who live outside of the big cities and who have had little direct experience with Communist activities, the illusion persists that Communists simply represent the extreme left of the radical-progressive-liberal camp. "We are the liberals and progressives," they say in effect, "who are satisfied with reforms and minor changes; to the left of us are the Socialists, who want to nationalize the means of production by democratic processes; and to the left of them are the Communists, who want to do the same thing but more or less along Russian lines." This, of course, is nonsense. Except for the slogans they make use of from time to time, the Communists have nothing in common with democratic Socialists or with liberals and progressives. They are reactionary in the same sense that fascists are re-actionary, for their aim is total power.

As things are today, wrong-headed tolerance of Communism is a less substantial evil than wrong-headed intolerance of people Senator McCarthy doesn't like. But the Retarded Liberals do do a certain amount of harm. In the first place, by making possible the existence of Fake Liberals, they provide a cover for Communist propaganda. In the second place, they make effective resistance to Communism more difficult. And in the third place, they create confusion at a time when clear thinking is our great need.

It is unneccessary, I hope, to say that I am not recom-mending that the *Nation* should be suppressed or banned or penalized in any way, nor am I suggesting that Retarded Liberals should be jailed or investigated. The Retarded Liberals—and, for that matter, the Fake Liberals too—should be free to say what they want to say. That is their right, just as it is our right to show what is wrong with what they say.

XII

The Great Reversal

Whittaker Chambers wrote a long book, *Witness*, to describe his two conversions—to Communism and from Communism —both of them emotional experiences of the highest intensity. Chambers was one of the few intellectuals who were attracted to the Communist party in the period between the Russian Revolution and the Great Depression. One day in 1925, while he was a student at Columbia University, he sat on a concrete bench on the campus, thinking about what he called to himself "the crisis of the twentieth century." He thought of the wars that were going on and the threat of greater wars, of the misery he had recently seen in Europe, of the emptiness and purposelessness of American life; and he thought, too, about what he had read in Marx and Lenin about the socialist state and the necessity for using dictatorship and terror to achieve it.

"When I rose from the bench," he writes, "I had decided to leave college for good and change the whole direction of my life. I had decided to join the Communist party." Why? Let him say:

The ultimate choice I made was not for a theory or a party. It was—and I submit that this is true for almost every man and woman who has made it—a choice against death and for life. I asked only the privilege of serving humbly and selflessly that force which from death could evoke life, that might save, as I then supposed, what was savable in a society that had lost the will to save itself. I was willing to accept Communism in whatever terms it presented itself, to follow the logic of its course wherever it might lead me, and to suffer the penalties without which nothing in life can be achieved. For it offered me what nothing else in the dying world had power to offer at the same intensity—faith and a vision, something for which to live and something for which to die. It demanded of me those things which have always stirred what is best in men—courage, poverty, self-sacrifice, discipline, intelligence, my life, and, at need, my death.

After twelve years, more than half of them spent in working with Soviet spies, Chambers turned against Communism as suddenly as he had turned toward it. Of course, as he admits, there had been preliminary doubts, but he can point to an exact moment when he said to himself, "This is evil, absolute evil. Of this evil I am a part." And from that moment he ceased to be a Communist.

What I had been fell from me like dirty rags. The rags that fell from me were not only Communism. What fell was the whole web of the materialist modern mind—the luminous shroud which it has spun about the spirit of man, paralyzing in the name of rationalism the instinct of his soul for God, denying in the name of knowledge the reality of the soul and its birthright in that mystery on which mere knowledge falters and shatters at every step. If I had rejected only Communism, I would have rejected only one political expression of the modern mind, the most logical because the most brutal in enforcing the myth of man's material perfectibility, the most persuasive because the least hypocritical in announcing its purpose and forcibly removing the obstacles to it. If I had rejected only Communism, I should have changed my faith;

I would not have changed the force that made it possible. I should have remained within that modern intellectual mood which gives birth to Communism, and denies the soul in the name of the mind, and the soul's salvation in suffering in the name of man's salvation here and now.

How far Chambers' rejection of "the materialist modern mind," the "modern intellectual mood," has carried him is not yet clear. But he is convinced that gradual socialism, such as the British Labour Party introduced in England, and re-formism, especially the reformism of the New Deal, are dangerous in the same way as Communism.

I saw that the New Deal was only superficially a reform move-ment. I had to acknowledge the truth of what its more forthright protagonists, sometimes unwarily, sometimes defiantly, averred: the New Deal was a genuine revolution, whose deepest purpose was not simply reform within existing traditions, but a basic change in the social and, above all, the power relationships within the nation. It was not a revolution by violence. It was a revolution by bookkeeping and lawmaking. In so far as it was successful, the power of politics had replaced the power of business. This is the basic power shift of all the revolutions of our time. This shift *was* the revolution.

Both of Mr. Chambers' conversions were more dramatic— more concentrated, so to speak—than anything I experienced, and I think that in that respect I am more representative of the ex-Communist intellectuals than he is. But what he went through on breaking with Communism is, in an intense form, what most of us went through. For anyone who knows Communism at first hand, neutrality is, at least in the long run, impossible: if you aren't for it, you have to be against it. Not only does the party deny neutrality in theory, recognizing only allies and enemies; in practice it eliminates the neutrals whenever it can. When anyone breaks with the party, he is at once denounced in the most abusive terms, even if his criticisms are fairly moderate, as mine were to begin with. The party knows well enough that the ex-Communist must become an anti-Communist.

To Chambers it was clear, as in a moment of revelation, that his renunciation of Communism had the most far-ranging philosophical and political implications. I, on the other hand, took months to come to terms with the intellectual consequences of my withdrawal from the party. When, moreover, the process of revaluation was completed, my position was not at all that taken by Mr. Chambers. Although I found myself, I believe, as uncompromising a foe of Communism as he, I was by no means ready to reject the rationalistic tradition of our modern era, and, far from regarding reformism of the New Deal type as an evil, I had come to regard it as the best available means for the salvaging of civilization. I had, in short, worked my way back in the direction of the liberalism from which I had started, but in the course of doing so I had learned to question many of the assumptions I had once made, and so I called myself a "critical liberal."

Chambers, however, is not the only ex-Communist to become an intransigent enemy of New Deal reformism, and the opposition of ex-Communists and former fellow travelers to all the policies associated with the names of President Roosevelt and President Truman is one of the significant facts of contemporary intellectual life. Think, for instance, of Max Eastman, who was a militant Socialist in the days before World War I and the guiding spirit of the *Masses* and its

successor, the *Liberator*. For some years after the Russian
Revolution he was one of the leading American spokesmen
for Soviet Communism, but in the later twenties, when the
great struggle for power was going on between Trotsky and
Stalin, he took the side of Trotsky, whom he knew and admired. His persistence in defending Trotsky after the latter
had been vanquished invited the denunciations of the victorious faction, the Stalinists. Eastman was quick to strike
back, and in the early thirties, when so many of us were just
beginning to be interested in Communism, he was a belligerent critic of Stalin's Russia and the Communist party of the
United States. Although he was anathema to me then, I realize now how close he was to being right. If I had had sense
enough to recognize the truth in his book about Soviet writers,
Artists in Uniform, I should have a good deal less now to look
back on with regret, but of course I succeeded in convincing
myself that it was all anti-Soviet propaganda. (And when
Eastman accused me—unjustly, as I thought then and still
think—of omissions and distortions in my biography of John
Reed, that didn't make me any more inclined to believe what
he was saying about Russia.)

As late as 1940 Eastman considered himself a Socialist,
though non-Marxist as well as anti-Stalinist. Subsequently,
however, he came to feel that any type of socialism would
result in tyranny, and he became increasingly distrustful of
New Deal reformism. What we have to worry about, he now
argues, is power. Before 1929, he admits, the power of Big
Business was excessive, but that has been checked, and we
should now be concerned with the power of the labor unions
and the farmers' pressure groups and especially the govern-

ment. If he is willing to grant that the New Deal was a good thing to begin with, he insists that it became a menace because the "socialist liberals," instead of stopping when a balance of power had been reached, went on "leading us in the direction of the slave state."

Like Chambers, Eastman feels that there are more than accidental resemblances between the New Dealers and the Communists. He sees a "large group of liberal-minded reformers, not pretending to be a class, not seizing the power but creeping into it, not smashing the state but bending it to their will." These reformers, he maintains, have too much in common with the Communists to be able to combat them effectively. In the spring of 1952 he wrote: "I think the incredible ineptitude of our foreign policy, or lack of it, springs from the same source. Its leaders are weak-willed and muddle-headed about the Soviet Union because its economic system represents their own ultimate ideal, and this taints their honest hatred of its political and cultural tyranny." It is not surprising that at that time Mr. Eastman was an apologist for Senator McCarthy.

John Dos Passos, one of the notable novelists of our time, has followed a similar path. Author of a bitter book about World War I, *Three Soldiers,* he was the perfect example of the independent radical of the twenties, dissatisfied, questioning, outspoken. Convinced that the two Massachusetts anarchists, Sacco and Vanzetti, were innocent of the crimes with which they were charged, he fought hard to save them from the electric chair, and when they were killed, he felt that everything that was decent in American life had suffered a defeat. ("America our nation has been beaten by strangers who have turned our language inside out who have taken the clean

words our fathers spoke and made them slimy and foul.")
Some drastic change seemed to him necessary, and he began
to listen to the Communists. When the depression came
along, he worked with the Communists in various organizations, and he was one of the fifty-two who signed the manifesto
for Foster and Ford.

Dos Passos's disillusionment with Stalinism began early,
but for some time he did not attack the Communists, and he
was by no means reconciled to capitalism. In 1937 he went
to Spain as an active sympathizer with the Loyalists. What he
saw there convinced him that the Communists were ruthlessly
pursuing their own ends and were as willing to kill non-
Stalinist allies as fascists. He put his indignation into a novel,
The Adventures of a Young Man, which showed the vicious-
ness of Communist tactics both in the United States and in
Spain.

In 1941 he said that the New Deal, "in spite of many wrong
roads taken," had been "productive of real living good in the
national life." But as time went on, it seemed to him that the
Roosevelt administration was growing too powerful. By 1945
he was critical of the government's policies at home and
abroad, and eventually he wrote a novel, *The Grand Design,*
in which he represented Roosevelt as a dictator and his associates as charlatans and demagogues. The Labour government in England and the Fair Deal in America came to seem
to him only slightly less tyrannical than the Soviet regime. He
stated that he was opposed to both Big Government and Big
Business, but he looked more and more favorably on private
enterprise. ("The untrammeled power of the ruling class in
the Soviet Union makes you wonder whether the profit mo-

tive is as bad as it has been painted.") When the Arts and
Letters Committee for Taft was formed in the spring of
1952, Dos Passos was one of three co-chairmen. Max Eastman,
incidentally, was a member, and Whittaker Chambers,
though not listed as belonging to the committee, was reported to have said that he favored Taft.

From my point of view there is nothing immoral or dishonest or intellectually disreputable in having supported the
late Senator Taft for the presidency, but when we find men
who thought of themselves as extreme radicals in the thirties
backing the conservative wing of the Republican party in the
fifties, we can't help wondering what has happened. In each of
the three instances discussed the driving force seems to be fear.
These men began, like some of the rest of us, by thinking that
Communism was right, and then they came to the conclusion,
again like some of the rest of us, that it was wrong and had
to be fought. But the more they have fought it, the bigger
and more frightening it has appeared to them, and the harder
it has become for them to distinguish between real dangers
and imaginary ones.

The danger of Communism is real enough, but it is a danger
that must be carefully analyzed if it is to be successfully combated. When Mr. Chambers says that, in breaking with Communism, he felt that he was taking the losing side, and that he
has seen no reason to revise his opinion, he makes us wonder
whether his judgment of the world situation is solidly founded
in rational examination of the facts. Of Dos Passos I have
said, in writing about his recent novels, that he seemed to be
suffering from shellshock. That wouldn't be surprising, for
he is a sensitive person, and he has taken part in one world

war, reported another, watched half a dozen revolutions, lived through the anguish of the great depression, and studied the horrors of fascism and Communism. If he feels that the world is crumbling around his ears, we can't blame him, but we may hesitate to follow his political lead.

I personally believe that the good in the New Deal and the Fair Deal outweighed the bad. The point is, however, that it is possible to believe—as millions of Americans did and do believe—that the bad outweighed the good, without going on to assert that the New and Fair Deals represented either actual or embryonic totalitarianism. In modern society there is always a threat of totalitarianism, for a highly industrialized nation cannot get along without a powerful central government, and where there is power there is danger. But was this danger acute under the New and Fair Deals? The proof that it wasn't lies in the fact that, after twenty years in office, the Democracts could be voted out, and power could be transferred to the Republicans, without the least disturbance or difficulty. (And I, a firm supporter of Adlai Stevenson, am inclined to say that it was worth losing the election to prove that point.)

The conclusions held by Chambers, Eastman, and Dos Passos are shared by a certain number of intellectuals, many of whom were favorably disposed toward Communism in the thirties. It is my contention that these people give as unreliable an account of our present situation as the Retarded Liberals and detract in the same way from the effective fight against Communism.

Let us look, for instance, at the *Freeman,* a bi-weekly magazine founded in 1950 with John Chamberlain and Henry

Hazlitt as editors and Suzanne LaFollette as managing editor. (There have been several shifts in personnel and policy since the magazine was launched, and in the winter of 1953 there was a major shake-up.) "On the positive side," the editors stated, "our function is to expound and apply our announced principles of traditional liberalism, voluntary cooperation and individual freedom. On the negative side, it is to expose the errors of coercionism and collectivism of all degrees—of statism, 'planning,' controlism, socialism, fascism and communism." The *Freeman* has performed both these functions, but with varying emphasis. After Mr. Chamberlain and Miss LaFollette left the staff in January 1953, and Henry Hazlitt became editor, the magazine devoted much of its space to setting forth the theory of private enterprise—old-fashioned Manchester liberalism as revived by Hayek and Von Mises. Before that time, however, it specialized in attacks on Roosevelt and Truman, and its hero was Senator McCarthy.

John Chamberlain was for a time a fellow traveler, as he admits—"I myself was taken in by the Communists in the nineteen thirties" — and in 1932 he published a book, *Farewell to Reform,* in which he announced that liberalism had failed and called for a revolution, peaceful if possible. His flirtation with Communism, however, did not last long. Miss LaFollette also has a long record of anti-Stalinism, but she was not so skeptical back in 1930–31, when the *New Freeman,* of which she was editor, published many pro-Communist articles. Both these editors, in other words, had in their own ways followed the Chambers–Eastman–Dos Passos trail.

Again I must insist that, far from deploring the intelligent expression of the conservative position, I welcome it, and there have been many articles in the *Freeman* that I have read with profit. Its editorial policy, however, especially in the Chamberlain–LaFollette period, was called in question by its excesses. In particular, though many other examples could be found, there was Mr. Chamberlain's enthusiasm for McCarthy. In a review of the Senator's book, *McCarthyism: the Fight for America,* Chamberlain spoke of its sober scholarship, and then went on to explain why McCarthy had been misunderstood:

The truth is that Joe McCarthy has learned more and more about his subject—the influence of communism on the foreign policy, the domestic politics and the culture of America—as he has gone along. When he first became aware of the workings of infiltrators, spies and fellow-traveling dupes, he was an unsophisticated young politician from the Middle West. Being a Leo Durocher–John McGraw sort of fellow, a take-charge guy, he fumed, bit his nails, and rushed out of the dugout to protest before a large crowd that some illegal spitballs and emery balls were being pitched by Lefty Lattimore. True, he hadn't seen Lattimore nick the ball on his spikes. But there were certainly some strange optical hijinks as Lefty's curve dipped over the outside corner of the plate.

The review, which so pleased Senator McCarthy that he used his franking privilege to send out copies of it, admitted that Lattimore might not be "top Soviet agent," but argued that a mistake of that kind was forgivable since he had been proved to have a pro-Soviet bias. Chamberlain also spoke of McCarthy's "use of sober arithmetic regarding questionable loyalty cases in the State Department" in his Wheeling speech. More than half the review, however, was not concerned with McCarthy or his book but with the way in which the Communists infiltrated American cultural life in the thirties—"the poisoning of the word." As I have already pointed out, Chamberlain's estimate of the extent of Communist influence in the Red Decade is on the lurid side. He has managed to give himself the jitters, and that is why he can be so complacent about McCarthy. The review, it must be said, did manage to show some restraint. "We sincerely hope," Chamberlain wrote at the end, "that Joe McCarthy will not attempt to take on a Senatorial Battle of the Books, which would involve destruction of the First Amendment to the Constitution. The job is one for journalism, and for journalism alone." When, however, McCarthy fired the first salvo of the Battle of the Books, in the course of his attack on the overseas libraries of the United States Information Service, the *Freeman* quickly came to his defense.

The editors of the *Freeman* are too smart to be taken in by the lies McCarthy tells, but they remain convinced that his motives are of the best and that the good he accomplishes is tremendous. When the Senator, just before the election of 1952, charged that certain of Adlai Stevenson's advisers were Communists, the *Freeman* ignored the misrepresentations and misquotations and contented itself with telling McCarthy how he could have done a better job. "The truth is," an editorial stated, "that Joe McCarthy picked some likely-looking targets but failed to hit them where they were really vulnerable." After pointing out that Arthur Schlesinger, Jr., Bernard DeVoto, and James Wechsler were not guilty of the crimes with which they were charged but were guilty of crimes that were just as reprehensible, the editorial concluded:

It was never necessary for Joe McCarthy to try to link Wechsler and the other serious thinkers around Adlai Stevenson to the

Kremlin. All he had to do was to show that they are men who are sicklied o'er by the pale cast of a thought that doubts the ability of the free man to look out for himself without being wet-nursed by a Big Government that may, in 1984, turn out to be a Big Brother: Orwell Style.

How does it happen that men of some intelligence can persistently disregard the damage that McCarthy is doing to freedom at home and to the American cause everywhere in the world? A quotation from another editorial may help us to understand:

Why do so many sincere anti-Communists hate Senator Joe McCarthy? Personally, we think it is a matter of pique or wounded amour propre. Here the boys, from Sidney Hook down to Arthur Schlesinger, had been carrying an anti-Stalinist torch, honorably but without any important results. Then a wild man from Wisconsin, a pop-off guy with a gift for dramatizing the issue, muscled in on what had been an intellectuals' preserve. Action followed. The role of the IPR was limned without mercy; the Great Dog Lattimore was forced to bay the red harvest moon; John Service departed from Foggy Bottom. It was enough to burn any good intellectual to see Joe carrying off something that had never been carried off before.

This editorial, underneath its facetiousness, tells us a good deal about the *Freeman*. The first thing one notices is the contempt for the intellectuals as a class, though the editors of and contributors to the magazine are, of course, all intellectuals. The glorification of the proletarian, which, as John Chamberlain would be the first to tell you, was one of the absurdities of the thirties, is here transformed into admiration for the man of action, the hard-hitting "take-charge guy" from Wisconsin. What the intellectuals have accomplished in the fight against Communism is minimized. It is nothing at all to have exposed the evils of Communism in magazines that reach millions of readers, as Hook has done in the *New York Times Sunday Magazine* and Schlesinger in *Life*. If, however, you can get two or three charges to stick, out of hundreds recklessly made, you are saving America. Like many of their fellow citizens, the editors of the *Freeman* have worked themselves up into such a state over the dangers of Communism that only the crudely melodramatic behavior of a McCarthy can give them emotional relief.

Because they have so much more faith in McCarthy's methods than they have in their own professed purpose of opposing sound ideas to unsound ones, the *Freeman*'s editors open its columns to a variety of heresy-hunters. According to these people, the Reds and Pinkos are everywhere, in the government, the schools, the churches, the magazines, and they are very powerful. An anti-Communist, Mr. Chamberlain says, "will still have difficulty getting work from the fashionable old-line press—say, the *New York Times Book Review,* or the *Saturday Review of Literature,* or the slicks." The anti-Communists, indeed, have a bad time of it, and the *Freeman* is always glad to listen to their woes. If a girl flunks a course at Vassar and chooses to say that it is because she believes in "God, Human Dignity, and the United States of America," the *Freeman* will publish her story. If a third-rate but popular novelist attributes her bad reviews to the Red conspiracy, the *Freeman* will agree that she is a heroine. "One way to judge the importance of a book on the Soviet conspiracy," according to Suzanne LaFollette, "is by the silence or hatchet work of metropolitan reviewers."

This is the exact counterpart of the Retarded Liberals'
melodramatic defiance of McCarthy. "The dangers that face
us are no greater and essentially no different from those facing
a soldier in battle," writes Miss Kirchwey in the *Nation*. "If
we are deliberately ruined and even if we lack bread," an-
nounces Taylor Caldwell in the *Freeman*, "we'll fight on."
(The *Freeman*'s heroics seem particularly ridiculous when in
every issue it carries three or four pages of institutional advertising from some of the biggest corporations in America.)

Nor is it difficult to find other parallels between the Retarded Liberals and the Panicky Conservatives. Both of them
thrive on moral indignation, probably the most satisfying emo-
tion known to the human species. The Panicky Conservatives
charge gallantly against a far-flung conspiracy of Reds and
Pinkos, letting the epithets fall where they may. The Retarded
Liberals engage in a last-ditch fight to protect democracy from
the almost triumphant hordes of the McCarthyites. Each
group has its own way of reading history: if, as already noted,
Matthew Josephson argues that the horrors of McCarthyism
far exceed the brutalities of the Palmer Red raids and the de-
portation frenzy, Max Eastman insists that, in comparison
with Palmer, McCarthy is a sissy. Young people, looking for a
cause as young people will do, and enlisting in one crusade or
the other, acquire in either case a myth that bears little relation to the facts of American history.

If the *Freeman* has in recent months crusaded less sensa-
tionally for McCarthyism, the Senator has not lacked spokesmen among the intellectuals, for the *American Mercury*,
which has gone through so many permutations since H. L.
Mencken cast it adrift, is now virtually the official organ of

McCarthyism. Among its contributing editors are Howard Rushmore, for some time a McCarthy investigator, and the Reverend J. B. Matthews, who, if the Senator had had his way, would have headed the McCarthy committee's staff. Dr. Matthews' notorious article on Communism and the Protestant clergy, which brought forth a rebuke from President Eisenhower, was only one of a series of pieces he had written for the *Mercury*. An earlier article, "Communists and the New Deal," began: "There were a thousand Alger Hisses in the government in the New Deal–Fair Deal era."

Perhaps it would be stretching the term to describe all the *Mercury*'s contributors as intellectuals, but many of them have a good enough claim to the title. James Burnham, for example, a professor of philosophy and the author of several well-known books, was once a member of the radical intelligentsia. Yet Professor Burnham is indistinguishable from other writers for the *Mercury*. For that matter, it is hard to distinguish him from McCarthy himself. His article on Adlai Stevenson's aides contained even more misstatements of fact than the Senator's television speech on the same subject.

What the Panicky Conservatives hope to achieve is hard to determine. From 1917 on, as we have seen, the Communists have been aided by the tactics used against them. The Lusk inquiry and the consequent expulsion from the New York State legislature of duly elected Socialist members, the anti-Communist and anti-labor riots and demonstrations, Attorney General Palmer's raids and deportations, these things led large numbers of liberals to come to the defense of the Communists and even to regard them as allies in the united front against the *status quo*. The recklessness of Martin Dies, when he was chairman of the House Committee on Un-American Activities, not only encouraged Communist sympathizers to believe they were right but also served to obscure the real dangers of Communism in the late thirties. The Communist party today would be even weaker than it is if it could not point to the perils of McCarthyism.

What is unique in the present situation is the fact that wrong-headed and dangerous ways of fighting Communism are being sanctioned and even encouraged by a group of intellectuals. That these intellectuals have every right to their conservative views goes without saying. They are entirely free to take their stand with Adam Smith or Robert Taft or anyone else. If they want to quarrel with the ideas of John Dewey or Bertrand Russell or Mr. Justice Holmes, no one will try to stop them. On the other hand, they do have responsibilities. They have a responsibility to truth, which they do not serve well when they defend or gloss over the lies of a McCarthy. They have a responsibility to clear thinking, which they betray by their vague and violent talk about a Pinko conspiracy. They have a responsibility to the anti-Communist cause, which they constantly injure with their exaggerations and their other excesses.

Many of them, as I have said, have had some first-hand experience with Communism. Are they now trying to prove, to themselves perhaps as well as to others, that they have become one hundred per cent respectable? Are they moved by a sense of guilt for their youthful indiscretions? Are they absolutists by temperament, so that, when they abandon the Communist system of absolutes, they must find another? As I point out in the next chapter, no single answer suffices. But we are less concerned now with causes than with results. These intellectuals have twice betrayed the principle of freedom of speech that is the basis of the intellectual life—once when they supported Communism and now as they support McCarthyism. For some of us one such betrayal seems more than enough for a lifetime.

XIII

Renegades and Informers

In 1945 Louis Budenz returned to the Catholic faith, breaking with the Communist party, of which he had been a prominent member for ten years. Since that time he has been a member of the faculty of Fordham University and has written three books on Communism, delivered countless lectures, and testified for many hours before federal and state investigating committees. According to his testimony before the New York State Board of Regents in January 1953, he generally receives twenty-five dollars a day when testifying. His lecture fees, he said, ran to more than four thousand dollars a year. His total income for the period of slightly more than seven years he put at seventy thousand dollars.

In other words, Mr. Budenz makes a profession of ex-Communism. That in itself is nothing against him; many people are well paid for doing what they believe to be their duty. Although Mr. Budenz has made statements about particular individuals that I am inclined to disbelieve, I am prepared to admit that he has aided the government in its fight against the Communist conspiracy, and that his lectures, though mostly directed to audiences that needed no convincing, may have contributed to the understanding of Communism.

But whatever can be said of Mr. Budenz, professional ex-

Communists have an unsavory reputation—and with some
reason. Dr. J. B. Matthews, who was never a party member
but served in party fronts—for example, as the first chairman of the League against War and Fascism—became chief
investigator for the Dies committee, and when that job
petered out, began writing on Communism for the Hearst
newspapers. He also was a favorite witness at state inquiries,
presumably on a per diem basis, and, as already narrated, I
encountered him at the festivities of the Canwell committee
in Seattle in 1948, accompanied by Howard Rushmore, who
moved directly from the *Daily Worker* to the Hearst papers.
As I studied reports of their testimony in the Seattle papers,
I could see what an acute temptation they were under to produce more and more sensational charges—a temptation that
neither one of them, so far as I could make out, was having
much success in resisting. When, in 1953, they emerged as
investigators for McCarthy and contributing editors of the
American Mercury, their chief asset was obviously this capacity for sensationalism.

Sometimes the testimony of ex-Communist witnesses has
been not merely sensational but demonstrably false, as in the
case, already mentioned, of George Hewitt's charges against
Professor Melvin Rader. Other ex-Communists have contra-
dicted themselves under oath, as, for example, Paul Crouch
did in presenting evidence with regard to Leon Keyserling,
President Truman's economic adviser. All this has tended
to discredit ex-Communists in the eyes of people who have
never had the slightest sympathy for Communism, and feeling
of that sort had a great deal to do with the widespread prejudice against Whittaker Chambers when he first denounced

Alger Hiss before the House Committee on Un-American Activities. Fortunately Chambers' testimony in the two Hiss trials, and especially his book, *Witness,* have helped many people to see the man in a different light.

Far from being a professional ex-Communist, Chambers, after leaving the party, made a remarkably successful career for himself as a journalist on *Time.* Here he combated Communism in an effective fashion in book reviews, articles on foreign affairs, and special features. The question constantly haunted him as to what he ought to do with the knowledge he had concerning Communist espionage in Washington, and after the Nazi-Soviet pact he gave A. A. Berle, then Assistant Secretary of State for security, the names of a dozen Communists in government bureaus. According to what Chambers later heard, Berle laid the information before President Roosevelt, who laughed at him. Chambers became convinced, as we have seen, that there was a fundamental similarity between Communism and the New Deal, and that that was why the New Dealers were not diligent in getting rid of Communists. It seems to me that there are more reasonable explanations, but I can understand why Chambers held this belief and why he felt that he must carry on the fight by himself. He did subsequently give information to the FBI, but it was not until the summer of 1948, when he was subpoenaed by the Committee on Un-American Activities, that his story became public.

What happened then is well known. Alger Hiss, who had left government employment to become president of the Carnegie Endowment for World Peace, categorically denied Chambers' charges and challenged him to repeat them outside the protection of Congressional immunity. Chambers did repeat them on a radio program, and Hiss sued for libel. Chambers was then summoned to appear before the grand jury that was currently looking into charges of Communist espionage, and as a result Hiss was indicted for perjury. In the first trial the jury disagreed, but in the second he was convicted.

The Hiss–Chambers case was not only one of the most dramatic incidents in recent American history; it changed the minds of a large and important section of the American people. The way in which most investigations of Communism had been handled had disgusted many people, so that they were willing to take the side of anybody who was charged with being a Communist. They—I could say we—refused to believe in the existence of Communist espionage on a large and dangerous scale, and such charges as Chambers was making seemed fantastic. In this particular instance, moreover, Hiss was vastly more presentable than his accuser, and that made it all the easier to believe in his innocence.

As the evidence piled up, however, it became more and more difficult to avoid the conclusion that Hiss was lying. And if he was lying, our whole conception of his character had to be revised, not merely because he had stolen government papers and turned them over to Soviet agents but also because he had accepted financial and moral support from a host of influential friends. (The parade of character witnesses, including two Justices of the Supreme Court, becomes, from Hiss's point of view, not theirs, one of the most cynical demonstrations ever maneuvered.) We were forced to Hamlet's conclusion—that a man can smile and smile and be a villain. For some the turning point was the Congressional investigation;

for myself the first trial; for others the second trial; for still others Chambers' book. But at one point or another we came to see the reality and the danger of the Communist conspiracy.

Other ex-Communists had been pushing us to the same conclusion, or were about to do so. In 1940 Benjamin Gitlow published *I Confess*. Gitlow, a left-wing Socialist in the period before World War I, was associated with John Reed in the founding of the Communist Labor Party. In 1919 he was picked up in a Lusk committee raid and was sent to prison for criminal anarchy. He was an active Communist throughout the twenties and was the party's candidate for vice-president in 1924 and 1928. Then in 1929 he and Jay Lovestone and the other members of their faction were read out of the party by Joseph Stalin himself. If Gitlow's book did not have much to tell about espionage, it did reveal the complete subordination of the American Communist party to the Russian government.

In 1947 Louis Budenz published *This Is My Story*. Budenz was active in the labor movement and the Socialist party in the twenties, and in the early thirties was national secretary of the Conference for Progressive Labor Action. Because of the depression in America and the triumph of fascism in Germany, he favored a united front that would include the Communists, and when, in 1935, the Communist party began to advocate the Popular Front, he became a party member. Because of his experience in labor activities and in journalism, he was a useful acquisition, and he was at once taken into the inner circle. For more than six years he was a member of the party's National Committee, and for some time he edited its official paper, *The Daily Worker*. Budenz's story shows how rapidly the Russification of the party proceeded after the Lovestone expulsion described by Gitlow, so that nominal leaders such as Earl Browder trembled at the least word from Russian representatives. And it shows, too, how the party was used as a recruiting center for Soviet spy rings.

Two books published in 1951 exposed the operations of these apparatuses. Vienna-born Hede Massing, who had testified against Hiss in his second trial, described in *This Deception* her activities as a courier or go-between, and Connecticut-born Elizabeth Bentley gave an account of similar activities in *Out of Bondage*. Miss Bentley's story is particularly interesting because, aside from her underground career, it seems so typical. In the winter of 1934–35, when she was worried about the depression and was lonely and unhappy, she drifted into one of the party fronts, the American League against War and Fascism. This organization gave her a sense of purpose and kept her busy, and it was an easy step into the party, of which, she discovered, many of her fellow workers in the league were members. Employed for a time by an Italian Fascist outfit, she found it natural, as an anti-Fascist, to pass on to the party any information she could pick up. Thus she got into the underground almost without knowing it, and when she fell in love with her "contact," Jacob Golos, who was nominally head of a travel organization called World Tourists, but was in fact a major figure in Soviet espionage, she was hopelessly entangled. It became her job to collect dues from Communists in Washington and to carry back to New York whatever government secrets they had been able to gather. Thus, when she decided to break with the party, she was able to give to the FBI the names of some thirty-five persons in government offices from whom she had received information.

There is great variation in these ex-Communist autobiographies, from Whittaker Chambers' intense and anguished soul-searchings and Ben Gitlow's plodding, factual narrative to Miss Bentley's brisk and superficial journalism. Each of them, however, has considerable importance. (The same cannot be said for Gitlow's sequel and Budenz's sequels.) Taken together, they demonstrate beyond any possibility of doubt that Soviet Russia has for many years maintained an elaborate espionage organization in this country and that it has recruited agents from the Communist party. Since, as I have been saying all along, espionage and conspiracy are the facts on which we must concentrate, the authors of these books—in differing degrees, to be sure—deserve our gratitude.

Yet the thing that makes the books important makes them unrepresentative. When Elizabeth Bentley was asked to become a courier, she was exalted. "Heretofore, like most American Communists, I had been playing at being a revolutionary," she writes; "now I was to become one in dead earnest." (Chambers had had the same feeling in 1932.) If espionage is the mark of the real revolutionary, then it is certainly true that most of the Americans—some hundreds of thousands, no doubt—who have belonged to the Communist party for longer or shorter periods of time in the thirty-five years of its existence have been playing.

Who were the Communists? Most of them in the thirties were people you might have known, perhaps did know— teachers, lawyers, social workers, booksellers, waiters, barbers, and drugstore clerks. Idealism, personal grievances, and a sense of insecurity mingled in them in strange combinations, but they were for the most part simple-minded people—suckers, in fact—who paid their party dues, bought party literature and sometimes read it, and did a lot of hard work in party fronts. Party organizers tolerated them, barely, because they brought in a little money, swelled party statistics, and took care of jobs that weren't important but had to be done. Besides, who could tell what valuable contact even the dumbest comrade might turn up with? In due season they became disillusioned, or maybe just peeved or bored. They dropped out and their defections were not lamented or even much thought about. Most of them went about whatever they were doing, without regrets, except perhaps for time and money wasted.

If it is important for people to realize that some Communists were spies, it is equally important for them to understand that most Communists weren't, for the failure to make that distinction is doing a lot of harm. Think, for instance, of Y, a member of the party branch to which I belonged at Harvard in 1938–39. He belonged to the party only that one year, and no one except the ten or twelve of us who were in the unit knew that he was a member. That spring he accepted an appointment at another university, and before he took up his duties there the Soviet-Nazi pact had been signed and he was fed up. There was nothing formal about his break with the party; he simply failed to make contact with the branch in the community to which he moved. It would have seemed silly to go around telling people that he had once been a Communist; he had made a clean break, and that was enough for him. Time passed, and he achieved some eminence in his profession and a reputation as an anti-Communist. And then suddenly, because of my testimony before the Velde committee, the papers were saying in large print that he had once been a Communist. It was true, of course, but the mood of 1953 scarcely permitted a just evaluation of the truth.

I have always been glad that I was an open member of the party, for that freed me from any temptation to conceal my past. Until recently, however, I have sympathized with those who did not reveal past party affiliation. It was not, I felt strongly, something to lie about, but I could not see that an ex-Communist was under any obligation to give himself away. I feel differently now. For one thing, what we have learned about Communist espionage provides some justification for the conviction, held by many members of Congress and a large section of the American people, that all the facts about Communist activity ought to be known. For another, the emphasis on espionage in recent books about Communism makes it desirable that the ex-Communists who were never spies should be heard from. Then perhaps people could realize that what Communism meant to Chambers and Budenz and Miss Bentley was not what it meant to the majority of those who are now ex-Communists.

This suggests that there should be some way in which ex-Communists could come clean, some way that would give them more protection than legislative investigations can provide. Arthur Hays Sulzberger, publisher of the *New York Times,* has proposed that an arbitrary date should be set—he suggests the beginning of the Berlin airlift in 1948—and that amnesty should be granted anyone who had quit the party before that date. This would be a step in the right direction, but, as Mr. Sulzberger admits, the administration of such a program would be full of difficulty. David Dubinsky, president of the International Ladies Garment Workers Union, has come up with a twofold proposal: first, a presidential commission to advise on all aspects of the problem of fighting Communism, at home and abroad; second, a privately sponsored information center that would work quietly to protect American institutions from infiltration. "This committee," according to Mr. Dubinsky, "would seek no headlines, would hunt down nobody, would propose no policies. It would act as a clearing house for all relevant data about Communist activity." Working together, the two organizations could find ways of implementing Mr. Sulzberger's suggestion.

But perhaps there is another way of getting at the problem. I wish there might be a League of ex-Communists devoted neither to repentance nor to self-justification but to the establishment of the truth. Such an organization, if it contained any considerable proportion of the ex-Communists, would be able to verify or disprove the claims of any but the most secret members of the party, whose cases ought in any circumstances to be investigated by the FBI. It would be in a position to welcome not only those who want to get rid of the burden of secrecy with regard to past affiliation but also those who have just broken with the party or are on the verge of breaking.

There is one obvious difficulty, and that is what might be called the kind of class feeling that exists among ex-Communists. The persons who were disillusioned in the late twenties are scornful of all the intellectuals who turned toward the party in the depression. Those who broke at the time of the Moscow trials feel superior to those of us who did not break until the Soviet-Nazi pact. We in our turn look down on later species of disillusionment. (I confess that I read with shocked incredulity Mr. Budenz's account of how he reconciled himself to the pact and to the reversal of June 1941.) And so it goes. But we were all suckers, no matter when we entered and when we departed from the party, and if the various groups could get together, they might discover that what they have in common—i.e., disillusionment with Communism—is more important than who got there first.

Perhaps, moreover, the League of ex-Communists might help to persuade the public to accept what seems to me axiomatic—that it is better for a man to be an ex-Communist than a Communist. Breaking with the party is never easy. I know, for I found the break a painful experience, in spite of the fact that I was praised rather than condemned by the public at large and in spite of the fact that most of my close friends in the party left it at the same time. Today the man who repudiates Communism faces not only loneliness and a long and difficult readjustment but also, unless he is willing to be the kind of ex-Communist Joe McCarthy approves of, a campaign of abuse and discrimination. Somehow we have to learn that, if we want to get people out of the Communist party, we must stop doing everything we can to keep them in. I am not suggesting that men and women should be praised for having been Communists, merely that they should not be penalized for no longer being Communists. Ex-Communists, as has been abundantly demonstrated, can be useful allies in the fight against Communism, and in any case the party is weakened by even a single defection. The Catholic Church has wisely cared for those former Communists who have returned to or accepted its faith, and in this respect those of us who are not Catholics might learn from the Church.

Finally, the League of Ex-Communists might succeed in clearing the air to such an extent that we could begin to think of something besides Communism. Writing in the *Freeman,* William Henry Chamberlin—himself a disillusioned fellow traveler, who achieved his disillusionment early and in the Soviet Union, and who has subsequently written with great insight on Soviet affairs—describes what he calls "Bankruptcy on the Left." His contention is that the whole radical–progressive tradition in America has been hopelessly contaminated by its involvement with Stalinism in the thirties. I agree that progressivism lost its bearings in the thirties, and I also agree that it is sterile today. But I am not willing to scrap our heritage from the liberals, reformers, progressives, and radicals of the pre-Communist era. Much can be salvaged if we can get to see the problem of Communism clearly.

It must be evident by now that I believe that the struggle against Communist espionage must be unremitting, and that Communist propaganda must be countered, the evasions of the Fake Liberals exposed, the mistakes of the Retarded Liberals analyzed. But I don't believe that this fight against Communism requires all our energies or that we can afford to give all our energies to it.

As I have tried to show, the very magazine for which Mr. Chamberlin is writing demonstrates that conservatism today is as bankrupt as the radical–progressive tradition he attacks, and for the same reason—its preoccupation with Communism. It is the rarest thing in the world for an idea to be examined on its own terms in the *Freeman.* The inevitable question is how it relates to Communism: is it for or against? The *Nation* is as bad in its obsession with what it denounces as the forces of reaction. And even those magazines that maintain a more judicious attitude toward Communism than either the *Freeman* or the *Nation* does seem to have little space for positive ideas.

The ex-Communist has, first of all, to come to terms with himself and with Communism, and that process ends, almost inevitably, by his becoming an anti-Communist. Too many of us have stopped there and thus have contributed to the present intellectual stagnation. That we should be preoccupied with Communism is natural, and yet we, more than others, ought to realize that anti-Communism is not enough. If we would look not merely at Russia but at the whole world, and if we would look at America and not merely at the American Communists, we might discover that there is a firm foundation on which we can build.

XIV

The Longer Look

In chapter VII, when I was talking about what we defend, I set forth our situation in the simplest possible terms: Russia's way of life is bad, and ours, by and large, is pretty good. Both propositions are true, but they do not contain all the truth there is nor all the truth we have to reckon with.

Today, when Communism is identified with Russia's aggressive totalitarianism, it is hard for us to remember that the Communist idea once expressed a great and generous hope for the welfare of mankind. The belief that human beings can shape the institutions under which they live has not always existed in the world, and it has really flourished only in the past two centuries. Our own American Revolution was a product of that belief and at the same time a great factor in its general acceptance. When Karl Marx and Friedrich Engels were growing up in the first part of the nineteenth century, there were many men in Europe and America who were intoxicated by this faith and were convinced that they could design perfect social institutions. Young Marx and Engels saw the element of fantasy in these schemes: if it was true that men could make institutions, it was also true that institutions made men. You could not step outside history, as the utopians were trying to do; you had to master history, and the only way to master it was to understand its laws.

We see now that there was also an element of fantasy in the ideas of Marx and Engels, as there always must be in the ideas of anyone who convinces himself that history embodies his will. But they knew more than the utopians, and they thought in larger terms. They saw, for instance, that science was transforming all patterns of thought, and they attempted to find a scientific foundation for their plans of social readjustment. (They were so convinced of their success that they arrogantly called their scheme of things Scientific Socialism.) They were quicker than most of their contemporaries to perceive the revolutionary importance of industrialism, and they based all their predictions on the belief that the process of industrialization would continue and would make possible an economy of abundance. They shared with the utopians a desire for not only political but also economic equality, and they foresaw, after the revolution and the dictatorship of the proletariat, the withering away of the state and the establishment of a perfect democracy in a classless society. They also foresaw the triumph of working-class solidarity over nationalist sentiments and thus the establishment of universal peace.

This is not the place to discuss the mistakes of Marx and Engels, except in so far as they help us to understand our present situation. Marx's analysis of capitalism, brilliant as in many respects it was, contained too many elements of wish fulfillment to be reliable. Capitalism had more vitality than he supposed, and the capitalists were more flexible. By and large, the rich did not get richer and the poor get poorer, though there were periods in which that seemed to be happening. In the more advanced industrial countries the workers

were able to win some part of the fruits of industrialism, and
the working class, in the main, preferred to fight for such
gains instead of striving for revolutionary change. Even the
millions of workers in European countries who called themselves Socialists and followers of Marx were only nominally
committed to a revolutionary seizure of power.

The revolution took place in a backward country—and because the country was backward. Lenin was a devout disciple
of Marx and Engels, but he was also a man of action, with an
intense loathing for Czarist tyranny. In Russia, backward not
only industrially but also politically, there was a strong con-
spiratorial tradition, and this permitted Lenin to form a small
but powerful party of professional revolutionaries. The Leninist conception of the disciplined party, which, as we have seen,
remains the ideal, though not always the practice, of Communists everywhere, was his great contribution to the shaping of
Communism as it is today. It enabled him to seize power at
a time when war had reduced Russia to chaos. Though he was
inferior to Marx as an economist and philosopher, Lenin had
proved himself to be a better revolutionary strategist.

Before we examine the consequences of Lenin's seizure of
power, we must note that Marx was also wrong in his estimate
of the strength of nationalist sentiment. Nationalism continued to grow in intensity, and in 1914, when the First World
War broke out, it was stronger than working-class solidarity.
The war itself proved a powerful stimulant to nationalism,
and in the period between the wars nationalism took on more
and more virulent forms. Even the rulers of Soviet Russia,
however much they were committed in theory to internation-

alism, found the nationalist appeal too strong to be neglected, and in the Second World War they used it for all it was worth.

Lenin immediately realized that the Soviet Union could survive in a hostile world and the promises of Communism be fulfilled, only if Russia were industrialized. What he did, and what Stalin did after him, was to use the power of the state to force industrialization, trying to accomplish in years what other countries had taken decades to do. This, in an important sense, is *the* revolution in Russia. From industrialization the people of Russia, who have paid a great price for it, have derived little profit, but Russia has become one of the two great powers in the world today.

From another point of view, the great significance of the Russian Revolution lies in the fact that so few people were able to gain control of a tremendous country. The problem of social control is one of the thorniest of our problems. Anyone who has had as much experience as I have with community projects is not likely to retain many illusions as to what can be accomplished by voluntary cooperation. People accomplish very little unless they are working under some sort of compulsion. In older, tribal societies, in which conditions changed little from generation to generation, much of the compulsion was furnished by tradition. The early civilizations, however, were all based on a simple form of compulsion, slavery, and without slavery the achievements of Egypt, Sumer, Babylon, Greece, and Rome would have been impossible. Feudal society rested on tradition and on the form of slavery known as serfdom. Only in modern times has there been a general assumption that people ought to be free to decide what they want to do.

Yet an industrial society requires a much higher degree of coordination than an agricultural society. Theoretically this is achieved under capitalism by the operation of the laws of supply and demand. Actually, as Marx delighted in pointing out, the establishment of industrialism in England was brought about by a violent form of coercion: the enclosure of the common lands, which created a proletariat that had to work in the factories or starve. Throughout the early history of industrialism, as Marx also insisted, governmental powers were used to make sure that large masses of people had no practical alternative to the long hours and poor pay of the factories. And if governments today, at least in the democracies, do not exercise that kind of compulsion, but, rather, intervene to protect the workers, the fact remains that we are a long way from laissez faire.

Modern industrial society requires an unparalleled concentration of power in the hands of government, and this is true whether a country is democratic or totalitarian, whether its economy is socialized or capitalistic or mixed. The important problem, of course, is whether power is limited or absolute. The power is going to be there in any case, but it makes a lot of difference to all of us whether the system of government provides for legal and peaceable means of taking power out of the hands of the people who happen to be exercising it at a particular moment, if the rest of us decide that they are acting against our interests.

Very often, in the modern world, such means do not exist. In Russia Lenin developed a technique for seizing and holding absolute power. Natives of other countries, with other ideals of government, were able to use almost the same technique. Mussolini adopted it in Italy in 1922 and Hitler in Germany in 1933. Hitler appealed to the dispossessed, the rootless, the frightened, and, like Lenin, he knew how to build his following into a disciplined party. Unlike Lenin, he was not restrained by a body of doctrine or a theory of history, and he was quick to use whatever sentiments would help his cause. He made nationalism a religion, and to nationalism he added racism. The frightened, resentful German people wanted something to hate, and Hitler gave them the Jews.

After examining the experiences of Russia, Italy, and Germany, we can only come to the conclusion that there is a totalitarian potential in modern society. A highly organized nation has real advantages in the world as it is, and this kind of organization can be most readily achieved by a dictatorship. Moreover, conditions in our society make it relatively easy for a dictator to seize power. In the first place, there is so much anxiety and so strong a sense of individual helplessness in our kind of society that an ambitious man, whether he is a fanatic or a sharp-witted demagogue, can build up a following. In the second place, the structure of our society is such that power is concentrated and therefore vulnerable. In the third place, when this ambitious man has got power, he can take steps, as we have seen, that will make it extremely difficult, for a time impossible, to dislodge him. Finally, by carefully using modern means and methods of propaganda, he can see to it that a lot of people don't want to dislodge him.

So far as this country is concerned, we can take satisfaction in the realization that totalitarianism has succeeded only in backward or handicapped nations. In the world situation, however, that is small comfort, for the world is full of backward and handicapped countries. Prewar Japan shows us that a country close to feudalism can simply take over Western techniques and, by blending Western nationalist sentiment with traditional loyalties, can forge its own variety of totalitarianism. If Russian Communism should vanish from the face of the earth tomorrow, we still could expect a series of totalitarian upheavals in Asia and Africa. The problem of China, the problem of India, the problem of South Africa, and a score of other problems would exist if Marx and Lenin and Stalin had never been born.

The new type of society has presented us in America with two sets of problems, external and internal. The great external problem at the moment is Russia, but, as we have just seen, a long line of problems lies beyond that one. The impetus acquired by science and industry is such that they appear certain to transform the entire world. This transformation could conceivably be accomplished peacefully, but at the moment there seems little hope that it will be, for industry and science carry with them the seeds of nationalism. The Western way of life has been spread through the world chiefly by conquest and exploitation, and sooner or later the backward peoples revolt against their colonial status. These revolts may be conducted in the name of democracy as well as in the name of nationalism. In fact, however, the backward peoples are seldom ready for democracy, whereas they take to nationalism with great ease. Consequently, as science and industry transform the world, rival nationalisms multiply and the danger of totalitarianism mounts.

For at least a century it has been apparent to most thoughtful persons that nationalism is incompatible with the conditions being created by science and industry. Our economic system is already worldwide in scope, and every day new inventions increase our interdependency. Obviously there can be no hope of peace until we have developed a political system that matches the economic system. But the advocates of world government cannot find much encouragement either at home or abroad. As matters stand, it seems likely that the political unification of the world will be accomplished, if at all, by a series of knock-down, drag-out fights among the principal contenders, beginning, of course, with the United States and Soviet Russia. Whether civilization can survive that process is, as everyone knows, problematic.

To some extent our ability to survive depends on our ability to meet our internal problems. I am thinking now not of economic and political problems, important as these are, but, rather, of the psychological and moral problems that are imposed on human beings by the kind of society that has grown up. The great British historian, Arnold Toynbee, maintains that Western civilization is, in essentials, re-enacting a drama that has already been played out some twenty times. With all due respect to Toynbee's erudition, I believe, as do most people, that the contemporary situation is new and different, though of course meaningful parallels with the past can be found. We, and I mean all the people of the world, are facing not only all the old problems but also some that have never been faced before.

To begin with, the unification of the world, which even Toynbee admits is something new, creates psychological as well as political problems. It is a fact that we have to live with every day. Our frontiers, which only yesterday were the Atlantic and the Pacific, are now on the Elbe, on the 38th parallel in Korea, and in the Straits of Formosa. The man you have lunch with today may be having lunch in Paris tomorrow, and the chances are that the young fellow at the filling station has seen military service in parts of the world you have scarcely heard of. And bombers can fly from here to there—and from there to here—wherever here and there may be. Nothing that happens anywhere in the world is irrelevant to us, as most of us are uncomfortably aware. It is a commonplace to say that the world has shrunk, but this means that the size of the world we have to take into account in our daily thinking has enormously expanded.

But the machine has changed more than the dimensions of our world; the quality of life is different in a society based on machinery and mass production. This is most apparent in one of the great modern cities, where millions of people are jammed together in physical proximity without having, without being able to have, any personal relationships. But the depersonalization of life is not merely an urban phenomenon, for the whole of life tends to be organized on the urban pattern. Even in a small town like my own, where personal relationships are still important, the sphere of impersonality constantly expands, as more and more people work in city factories, become dependent on automobiles and electricity, and get their entertainment—and most of their ideas about how life ought to be lived—from New York City and Hollywood. This is not the way the human species has been accustomed to live. Even as late as 1600, cities of more than one hundred thousand population were rarities, and most people never came near the cities and were little influenced by them. During most of human history life has been lived in small-town, almost in tribal, terms, and it is no wonder that we have trouble in adjusting ourselves to the complexity and impersonality of the great society. Each new invention is not only a problem in itself; it creates a new problem in human relations.

The complexity of the great society is responsible for the widespread feeling that ours is a civilization without values. Actually, of course, our society offers the individual a vaster range of values than any society that has hitherto existed. What worries us is the fact that the other fellow doesn't recognize our values as his values. Not only in primitive societies but in almost all pre-industrial cultures, values were traditional. The individual was trained in them from birth, and they were as much a part of his world as light and dark, as air and land and water. He might never in his lifetime come in contact with anyone who held different values, and if he did encounter such a monster, he could take care of him by labeling him as a barbarian or a heathen. Conflicts of interests there must always have been, but conflicts of values were rare.

In the great society, on the other hand, we have increasingly had to come to terms with people whose meat is our poison. For many of us, because of the shrinking of the world, this is a matter of physical contact, but the most habitual stay-at-home has to reckon with the mores of tribesmen in the heart of Africa. We have our own terms for disposing of outsiders —wops and kikes and niggers and gooks—but the magic has gone out of them. Little as some of us may like it, these people are part of our world, and we cannot get rid of them by calling names. Meanwhile historians and anthropologists reveal to us the diversity of the past, until we realize that there is nothing we consider good that hasn't at some time in some place been considered bad and nothing bad that hasn't been found good. We may if we choose cling to our faith in the absolute validity of our values, but we know that we cannot expect other people to agree.

Even in terms of our own country the area of shared values grows smaller and smaller. The values of earlier societies seemed permanent, being handed on from generation to generation, because modes of life changed slowly in the course of decades or even centuries. Men had plenty of time in which to adjust to the discovery of fire or the domestication of animals or the invention of the wheel. Today changes almost as drastic as these take place every year or so. A man who, like myself, has grown up with the century has lived through two revolutions in transportation: the development of the automobile from a rich man's toy to one of the necessities of life, and the whole history of flight. He has witnessed three revolutions in communications: the widespread adoption of telephones, the radio, and television; and three revolutions in entertainment: the movies, and again radio and television. He has seen electricity take the place of steam as the principal source of industrial power, and he has lived in the beginning of the atomic age. To each of these revolutions—and there have been dozens more of comparable importance—every individual has had to adapt himself as best he could; there has been no opportunity for a gradual communal adaptation to the new way of life.

Furthermore, the very process by which the great society came to birth involved the dissolution of traditional values.

The human reason, ever since its emancipation in the Renaissance, has been probing away at the secrets of the universe, and the more it has learned, the less certainty it has found. The universe as we now know it stretches out for billions of light-years, and we have discovered enough about the atoms out of which it is made to use them in blowing up cities—and perhaps the world. It is a universe that cannot easily be reconciled with the teachings of any of the world's religions, nor does it help us much when we try to determine what our values ought to be. Our values have to be forged in a universe that we cannot believe to be especially concerned with us, as individuals or even as a species.

Yet, in spite of everything, we do have a pretty good idea of where we stand. Science and industry have extended man's control over his environment, and there are not many persons who would choose to relinquish any of the gains that have been won. The most nostalgic old-timer in my town would not consent to live as his grandfather lived, on a monotonous, unhealthy, and not always adequate diet, paid for by long hours of the hardest labor. He would not give up his car, his electricity, his telephone, his television set. Least of all would he surrender the relief and the healing brought by the drugs and the skills of modern medicine. Science and industry hold out to men everywhere the promise of the abolition of poverty and disease, the amelioration of the struggle to survive, and even a few of the luxuries, and men everywhere are reaching out for those boons.

We know equally well what our dangers are. Since power is always power for both good and evil, man's increasing control over his environment means that as we fear nature less we fear man more. The most obvious of our dangers is war, for we have learned to destroy on as mighty a scale as we have learned to produce. The second great danger is the abuse of power, always present in minor forms, always threatening as a major catastrophe because of what I have called the totalitarian potential in our social structure. Finally, there is the related danger of a social crack-up under the strain of adjustment to a situation that never ceases to change.

If we take a long look, it does not seem unreasonable to say that there is a close relationship between what has been happening in Russia and what has been happening in the United States, for in both countries we see manifestations of a change that is worldwide. Does this mean that it makes no difference to the rest of the world which prevails in the struggle that is going on between them? In a sense, no doubt, it means just that, for world change will go on whichever wins, unless civilization is wiped out. On the other hand, there will be an incalculable difference in the way the change is brought about.

What I am saying is that the modern revolution is more likely to develop in humanly advantageous ways, ways bringing advantage to all the peoples of the world, in America and under American leadership than it is in Russia and under Russian leadership. This is not because Americans are better people than Russians but because of differences in Russian history and American history. Because Russia was a backward nation, the revolution there could take only a violent and tyrannical form. The leaders of the revolution could neither satisfy their own lust for power nor transform the nation's economy without enslaving and degrading the people.

The United States, on the other hand, has been as fortunate

as Russia has been unfortunate. Settled at a time when great changes were taking place in Western Europe, it offered a free field for experiment. The absence of an aristocracy and the existence of unlimited land encouraged the application of those democratic principles about which European thinkers were speculating. The country's resources not only permitted the rapid development of industrialism but also insured the nation's growth to the status of a great power. Until recent decades the oceans constituted a sufficient barrier against hostile nations. Here if anywhere Western man had a chance to show what he could do.

The results are less than utopian, but if we look at them carefully, we find that they are not altogether discouraging. We have not only achieved the highest productivity in the world; we have achieved, as I was arguing in the last chapter, a more equitable distribution of wealth. Our rough-and-ready democracy, in spite of increasing pressures, continues to function. Our material prosperity is the envy of the world. Finally, there is some evidence that we are developing a new kind of culture. If so, this is important, for we may find here some indication of what the revolution through which we are passing may mean to mankind.

XV

The Way We Live Now

Wherever you are in America, you have only to open your eyes to see evidence of the transformation of our society. Here in Roxborough the evidence begins within sight of my study window, from which I look across lawn and flower garden to forest. For over one hundred years this was a farm, supporting four generations of Norths and Cutters, and when Roxborough's population was at its peak, in the middle of the nineteenth century, it was one of hundreds of farms in the town. Today there aren't half a dozen men in the whole of Roxborough who get the major part of their livelihood from farming. We have our kitchen gardens, and some of us have hens, and here and there a family keeps a cow, but most of what we eat comes from the counters and shelves of supermarkets. Our clothing is selected from mail-order catalogues or bought in city stores, and the spinning wheels and looms and hatchels of our ancestors are bait for the antique dealers. The fuel we burn is delivered in trucks, and wood for the fireplace is hard to come by and almost as dear as in the cities.

These, of course, are signs of a two-way revolution. The farming is now done elsewhere, and done with fewer men and more and more machines, under conditions that often approximate the conditions of the mass-production industries.

We live in the country, but we live on the produce of California and Texas and Florida and New Jersey, just as we would if we lived in Troy or Albany or New York City. And by and large we make our living out of industry, most of us directly, by working in the factories of the Capital District, most of the others indirectly, by catering to the summer people and the tourists or serving the needs of the commuters. The small town has been absorbed by the great society.

The kind of life we lead is made possible by a series of machines, just as it would be if we lived in a city, the only difference being that most of the machines are owned by us individually instead of being parts of a gigantic impersonal apparatus. The apartment dweller takes for granted water and sanitation and light and heat and transportation, whereas these are matters that we have to take care of ourselves. Even at that, we are in much the same situation as millions of people who live in the housing developments that have multiplied on the fringes of the cities, and we are closer to the apartment dwellers than we are to the people who lived on these acres twenty-five years ago.

Counting cars, pumps, lawnmower, refrigerator, vacuum cleaner, and so forth, our family has at its disposal at least a dozen motors, and our neighbors have as many or more. For most people in the town the automobile is the indispensable machine, for it is what makes it possible for them not to have to choose between working in the city and living in the country. If you drive into Troy between six and eight in the morning, or if you drive out from Troy between four and six in the afternoon, you get the feeling that all Roxborough is on the move. But a car is not merely a key to a job; for us in Roxborough, as for millions of Americans, it is the foundation of our social life, and we drive in it both for recreation and to get to the places where recreation, of the kind we happen to be seeking, can be found. For us, as for millions, it has altered the mores of courtship and sex, and it is with respect to the use of the car or the cars that a major part of family life has to be planned. Moreover, for those who know something about machinery, and they are numerous in Roxborough, it is a focus of intellectual interest and one of the livelier topics of conversation.

Next to the automobile, it is electricity that has revolutionized Roxborough. The first power lines were run into the town barely twenty-five years ago, against fanatical opposition. We ourselves, because we were a long way from the main line, spent several summers and two winters here without electricity. Kerosene lamps were no novelty to my wife and me, for we had grown up with them, and we remembered the excitement of getting electric lights. That was what electricity meant at the time of the First World War—more adequate, more convenient lighting. But by 1938, when electricity was coaxed by subsidies up our road, it brought release from a dozen kinds of drudgery by way of the automatic water pump, the refrigerator, the washing machine, and other ingenious devices. As the power lines have pushed farther and farther back into the hills since World War II, they have carried all these conveniences and new means of entertainment as well. When power fails, it is, many people say, the television that they miss most. If we are happy enough without TV, we do miss the record-player and the FM radio.

As anybody can see, rural life more and more closely resembles urban life, and this is true not only for small towns like ours, which has become a semi-suburb, but also for the areas that raise the nation's food. In the dairy country of western New York, in the Corn Belt, in the Wheat Belt, in the fruit-raising sections of California and Florida, farmers not only have thousands of dollars worth of labor-saving machinery in their barns and fields; they have conveniences and luxuries in their homes. Even in the poorer farm country the automobile and electricity are remaking the pattern of rural life.

Naturally the conveniences and luxuries have to be paid for, and they wouldn't be available if people couldn't buy them. The revolution, in other words, is economic as well as technological. During the worst years of the depression we were spending summers in Roxborough and winters in the city, and we could see that the victims of the depression fared better in Roxborough. The city jobless had nothing, but in Roxborough a man without a job could raise some food, cut some wood, do a little tinkering here and there. He was better off not only because he and his family ate more adequately but also because he had something to do. If a depression should come along now, we in Roxborough would still be better fixed, but we should have more to lose than did the people who were living here in 1930. That is part of the price we pay for being absorbed by the great society.

What we have gained, on the other hand, will not be underestimated by someone who has been looking at the town for twenty years. As I said at the beginning of this book, the effect of prosperity is to be measured not merely in terms of motors and gadgets but also in terms of human satisfactions. Men, well paid, able to live comfortably, have more self-respect. Women, released from part of their drudgery, with a little leisure, and money enough to enjoy it, seem younger and prettier. Men, women, and children look better and obviously feel better, for they eat more nourishing food and can afford to go to doctors and dentists. If a TV set or a new car seems more important to a lot of people than dental repairs or a coat of paint on the house, most of them get around to the dentistry and the paint sooner or later.

You feel the difference whenever you see the town in action. An election used to be a depressing occasion, for it brought to light many fellow townsmen who ordinarily lived in backwoods obscurity. They were mostly ill at ease as they exercised their rights as citizens, and some of them were obviously hoping for a modest bribe. Today, though most of the men come to the polls in their work clothes, they have an air of self-assurance that no one can miss. Some of us sell tags on election day for the benefit of the town library, and though only a tenth of the people use the library, almost everybody drops coins into the boxes, and not a few give bills.

If you were to drive by the town hall some night when the fire company was meeting, you would notice that the cars parked outside are recent models in good condition. Although most of the volunteer firemen are factory workers, we do have a college professor, a salesman, an office manager, and a couple of other white-collar workers, but you couldn't tell which is which by looking at the automobiles they drive. Nor could you judge as much as you might think from their clothes, for the college professor, having worked for a couple of hours on his plumbing, might be wearing greasy jeans, while the garage mechanic might have changed his clothes for a party.

If you listened in on a serious discussion, you could identify the various levels of education without much trouble, but even so you might be struck by the community, rather than the diversity, of interests.

When we first came to Roxborough, it was essentially a one-class town, a town that had been going downhill in population and industry for several decades and had no really rich people left in it. Although everybody was affected by the depression, some were harder hit than others, and incomes ranged from a moderately comfortable figure to near starvation level, but social status seemed to have little to do with earnings. As I said in *Small Town,* some people were regarded as socially inferior, but this was a moral rather than an economic judgment. If you were doing the best you could, you were as good as the next fellow.

Today the social composition of Roxborough is more complicated than it was twenty years ago, both because so many natives have been drawn into the urban whirlpool and because the town has become a semisuburb. In the latter process we have acquired not only factory workers but also white-collar workers, professionals, and a few managers and entrepreneurs. Yet class stratification hasn't taken place. There hasn't even been an alignment of newcomers versus natives, presumably because most of the newcomers have the same kind of jobs and earn the same kind of money as most of the natives and have had about the same degree of the same sort of education. The newcomers as a rule are young, and they don't differ much from natives of their age.

The professionals, to be sure, have more education, if not more money, but they show little tendency to stick together.

Like any other town, Roxborough is full of cliques, but their composition is constantly shifting, and they seldom seem to be determined by the jobs or the incomes or the education of their members. A few years ago an active clique of young couples was composed of two factory workers and a garage mechanic, all natives, and a white-collar worker, a newcomer. At a New Year's Eve party we had as guests an engineer, a photographer, a white-collar worker, a salesman, a garage mechanic, an undertaker, and their wives, one of whom was a teacher and another an insurance agent. It is true that the professionals sometimes entertain other professionals from the city or from other suburbs, but a party made up of townspeople is always a mixed affair.

The blurring of class lines is not peculiar to Roxborough; it reflects something that is happening to America. The breaking down of class distinctions, as has often been pointed out, is most evident in the matter of clothes. In the autumn of 1952 I went to a Stevenson rally in Troy, and from the applause I gathered that a large part of the audience was made up of union members, but it was impossible to tell from the way people were dressed who was a factory worker, who was a white-collar worker, and who belonged to a profession. Part of the explanation lies in the fact that factory workers now have money to spend on clothes, but that isn't the whole story. By and large it is considered improper in our society today to use clothes as a sign of social status or even, in the daily routine, of wealth. Clothes that served a symbolic purpose— the top hat, the frock coat, the starched shirt—have almost completely disappeared, and formal dress has become less common and less formal. Not only do Americans of all classes look much the same when they dress up; they are indistinguishable when they are not dressed up, and that is a larger and larger part of the time. If it takes a sharp eye to tell an original evening gown from an expensive imitation and the expensive imitation from a model that can be purchased by any shopgirl, it is almost impossible to tell the rich girl from the poor one when both are wearing blue jeans.

During the First World War newspapers excitedly reported that shipyard riveters and other workers in the money were buying silk shirts at five and six dollars apiece. This, editors assumed, demonstrated that the workers were overpaid, that they didn't know how to spend money, and, most important of all, that they were forgetting their place. One cannot imagine any kind of sartorial extravagance that would have created a comparable furor in World War II. A few conventions persist. White-collar workers usually wear collars and ties, though not always jackets. (Shopping in a large department store one summer day, I observed that jackets were obligatory for department managers but not for ordinary salesmen.) There are restaurants that won't serve a man who isn't wearing a coat and tie, and restaurants that won't serve women wearing slacks or shorts. (On the other hand, even expensive restaurants lying along main tourist routes are likely to advertise "Come as you are.") These conventions are vestigial. More and more, people can dress as they please, and differences grow out of individual tastes rather than social distinctions. Even expensive clothes, though their expensiveness may be obvious to those in the know, do not say to economic inferiors, as clothes used to, "I am different from and better than you."

In the more stable societies of the past, class differences were generally accepted, and there were recognized ways in which they were symbolized. We Americans have never been wholly at ease with such symbols, and probably that is why at certain periods so much emphasis has been laid upon them. After the Civil War, when great fortunes were being made, the newly rich found it imperative to display their wealth, and we entered upon a period of what Thorstein Veblen called conspicuous consumption. When a man made a million, he built an ostentatious house that was too large for his family and staffed it with more servants than he needed. As his wealth grew, his carriages, his private car, his yacht, his clothes, his wife's clothes, his art collection, his philanthropies, everything about him proclaimed the fact that he had money.

Today the conspicuous consumers are not the industrialists and financiers but the stars of movies and radio and the members of the expense-account aristocracy. And though many people envy these publicized figures their swimming pools and their night-club glamour and extravagance, almost everyone is aware that their wealth doesn't mean much, that it is almost as accidental as the prosperity of the winner of the Irish Sweepstakes or the sobbing beneficiary of "Strike It Rich" or some other giveaway program. These are not our masters; they are, on the contrary, our pets, whom we have chosen to pamper.

Although there are fewer very poor and, relatively speaking, fewer very rich than there were twenty-five or fifty years ago, there are still grievous economic inequalities in this country, but they don't seem so important as they once did. That is partly because almost all of us are better off than we were and therefore aren't so bitter against those who are still better off. It is partly because we know that the rich are heavily taxed and that their powers are curbed in many ways. And it is partly because the rich, instead of flaunting their economic superiority, seem a little embarrassed about it and try to assure us that they aren't any different from us. So we go about our various businesses with no feeling of inferiority and little resentment.

Most of the able-bodied men in Roxborough, as I have said, work in factories. Unless they are on shifts, they go to work early, but they also get home early. They work forty or forty-four hours a week, instead of the fifty-four or sixty or seventy-two hours that were common in the nineteenth century and persisted into the twentieth. Many of them are engaged in work that taxes body and mind, but in this time of full employment a man's nose can't be kept on the grindstone all through the working day. A man is likely to get a break for coffee, and if he goes to the toilet and sneaks a cigarette, he isn't going to be fired. When our Roxborough people come home, they aren't exhausted, but are ready to work around the house—practically every man in town has a dozen home-repair jobs that his conscience and his wife are nagging him to finish—or go to a party or a square dance or settle in for an evening with TV. Almost everybody is in debt, for no one makes enough to pay for all the things he and his wife and children want, but it is comparatively seldom that a car or a television set is repossessed. These people are getting a share of the good things of life, and they know it.

To the responsibilities and obligations of the great society most of them give little thought. They pay their union dues

as automatically, and, when they think about it, as resent-
fully, as they pay their income taxes. For the most part they
regard both government and unions as necessary evils, and
they are more conscious of both than they are of the higher
levels of management and ownership. They feel no animosity
toward the remote big shots, for they are scarcely aware of
their existence. Their gripes are over little things—the un-
reasonableness of a foreman, the stupidity of a fellow worker,
the cost and quality of food in the cafeteria. Few of them, so
far as I can tell, find acute satisfaction in their work, and yet
no one feels that his job is meaningless drudgery. (When a
man feels that way today, he goes and gets another job.) Any
job that I hear talk about calls for the exercise of some skill
that entitles a man to the respect of his companions and to
self-respect. And even when the day's work is pretty tedious,
a time comes when a man can go home to race motorcycles or
paint the house or make love to his wife.

For the women of Roxborough the revolution has been
even more of a success. To begin with, if they need or want
to work, there are jobs for them, and a great variety of jobs.
Most women under fifty in Roxborough have held jobs at one
time or another, and a considerable proportion are holding
jobs now. A girl expects to work before she is married and
perhaps for a year or two afterward, but she rarely thinks of
herself as having a career, and she has no regrets about quitting work when she starts to have a family. If she goes back to
work when her children are old enough to do without her, it
is more often because she is bored than because her earnings
are indispensable.

What makes the big difference for most Roxborough

women is the revolution that has taken place in their homes through their acquisition of labor-saving machinery. It has been a rapid revolution everywhere, and in Roxborough it has largely come about in ten or a dozen years. We have leaped almost in a single bound from an era in which a woman had to carry water, sweep and beat her rugs, scrub the family washing, and keep food in the spring house, into an era of multiple mechanical servants. Unless she has young children, a Roxborough woman enjoys hours of daily leisure, hours in which, of course, she may be very busy, but not under the old compulsions.

Here again it is true not only that the conditions of rural life approach those of urban life but also that the differences between classes are diminishing. When I was a boy, a woman didn't consider herself really well off unless her husband could afford to hire at least one domestic servant. Working-class families, to be sure, did not have servants, nor did the lower ranks of the middle class, but in business and the professions a man hadn't arrived if his wife had to do all her own housework. Today, with so many better-paid and otherwise more attractive jobs open to women, domestic labor has become a major luxury. Higher and higher in the social and financial scale women are relying on machines, just as the Roxborough women do, to lighten their burdens and give them leisure.

The formal political equality granted by the Nineteenth Amendment and the approximation of economic equality created by full employment have been accompanied by drastic changes in manners. Throughout all the fanciful shifts in fashion since World War I the freedom of women to dress so as to be able to do whatever they want to do has persisted. The freedom from gentility has spread upward from the working class, and perhaps downward from high society, wiping away many of the conventions by which middle-class women were enslaved. At the same time, thanks to better contraceptive methods and wider knowledge of their use, fewer women have to choose between constant pregnancy and abortion. And if we can believe Dr. Kinsey, women are achieving greater sexual satisfaction both in and out of marriage.

Let us try to add it all up. This is a prosperous society, with a larger and larger proportion of the people sharing in the prosperity. Distinctions diminish between country and city, between rich and poor, between men and women, between old families and the children of immigrants, even—though there is so much more to be desired—between Negro and white.

In *Democracy in America* Alexis de Tocqueville wrote:

> The good things and the evils of life are more equally distrib-
> uted in the world: great wealth tends to disappear, the number
> of small fortunes to increase; desires and gratifications are multi-
> plied, but extraordinary prosperity and irremediable penury are
> alike unknown. The sentiment of ambition is universal, but the
> scope of ambition is seldom vast. . . . Human existence becomes
> longer, and property more secure: life is not adorned with brilliant
> trophies, but it is extremely easy and tranquil. Few pleasures are
> either very refined or very coarse; and highly polished manners
> are as uncommon as great brutality of taste. . . . Almost all ex-
> tremes are softened or blunted: all that was most prominent is
> superseded by some mean term, at once less lofty and less low, less
> brilliant and less obscure, than what before existed in the world.

It was in 1831 that de Tocqueville visited the United States, but much of what he wrote fits our revolution. In the second half of the nineteenth century, with the expansion of industry, it appeared that de Tocqueville had been a poor prophet, for differences between rich and poor were constantly becoming greater, and equality of opportunity seemed to be a myth. That was the theme of much of the agitation of the period: the promise of American life had been betrayed. But now, with the industrial revolution in a later phase, de Tocqueville's predictions seem to be coming true. If in our day we tend to overstate the degree of equality, as certainly he did in his, the contrast between what we have and what the world has generally known can scarcely be exaggerated.

Although he believed that the world-wide triumph of democracy was inevitable and was on the whole a good thing, de Tocqueville, it will be recalled, was not unqualifiedly enthusiastic about the new order. Immediately after the passage I have quoted he wrote, "When I survey this countless multitude of beings, shaped in each other's likeness, amid whom nothing rises and nothing falls, the sight of such universal uniformity saddens and chills me, and I am tempted to regret that state of society which has ceased to be." The nightmare of "universal uniformity" has haunted critics of democracy ever since, and we still hear voices, some American, some European, complaining of the standardization of life in the United States.

American democracy is open to many criticisms, including many of those expressed by de Tocqueville more than a hundred years ago, but the charge of standardization will not hold water. As the experience of totalitarian countries ought to teach us, it takes a lot of doing to standardize human beings even in a slave state, and in a free state it is impossible. The individual may be standardized in a stable, stratified society, but in a social order that is constantly changing he cannot be. You cannot make people alike by giving them more and more opportunities to be different.

A quarter of a century ago, as mass production got under way, the assembly lines devised by efficiency engineers threatened what seemed to be an intolerable standardization of labor. Man was treated as a machine, not as a human being. But it soon became clear that it was more economical, as well as more humane, to treat machines as machines and men as men. Purely mechanical labor can always be done more cheaply by machines, freeing human beings for the more varied and more creative tasks that the machines cannot perform. Furthermore, through their unions and their individual acts of self-assertion, human beings find ways of resisting the tyranny and monotony of the assembly line. And so long as he has leisure, no man is likely to become a robot; even the man who performs one simple function all through the working day turns into a jack of all trades when he gets home.

The standardization of the product is the basis of modern industry, and sometimes the effects are good and sometimes they are bad, but even when they are bad, a remedy for the evil is likely to appear. If bakers succeed in foisting upon the nation a uniformly tasteless loaf of bread, smaller bakers emerge to furnish better bread for those who are willing to pay for it, and more housewives spend some of their leisure in doing their own baking. One supermarket is much like another, but any supermarket has a variety of goods on its shelves that would dumfound the corner grocer of a generation ago. And the magazines that are sold in the supermarkets indicate that the diet of the average American is more and more varied, experimental, cosmopolitan. Sometimes, indeed, it appears that we are on the way to becoming a nation of gourmets.

What is true of food is true of most of the other products of modern industry. The housing shortage that resulted from the depression and the war has led in these times of rising costs to the mass production of houses, usually badly built, ugly, and all pretty much alike. Even at their worst, however, such houses are preferable to the old-fashioned tenements of the factory towns, and there is no doubt that mass production could do a lot better than it is doing now. Furthermore, the growth of Roxborough is proof that a lot of people don't want to live in housing projects, and, thanks to the automobile, they don't have to.

It is in mass entertainment that many critics have found the greatest threat of standardization—movies, radio, television. Unquestionably these media have introduced an element of uniformity in American life: they give us our heroes, our catch phrases, our jokes; they influence our tastes and values. Very possibly this degree of uniformity is not a bad thing, even though it is accomplished on a low cultural level; it helps to hold the nation together. But in any case what the critics forget is that these media increasingly cater to a diversity of tastes and that through such by-products as the long-playing record they have enriched the lives of those who happen not to want what the millions want.

The way we Americans spend our leisure time is the best proof that standardization is a myth. The critic will point out that hobbies themselves are constantly being standardized, and that is true: as soon as people are interested in model railroads or sports cars or "Hi-Fi" sets or whatever it may be, societies grow up to organize these hobbies and businesses to exploit them. But that does not do away with the fact of diversity. How do you suppose the people of Roxborough are entertaining themselves this weekend? They are not all watching TV, though probably more are doing that than any other one thing; they are not all out riding in their automobiles, though that, too, is one of the more popular forms of diversion; they are gardening, bird-watching, tinkering with machinery, painting landscapes, listening to symphonies, restoring antiques, dancing, even reading books. You cannot see them without knowing that these are people who have multitudinous choices and are happy in that fact.

Perhaps it is a law of industrial development that machines first enslave men and then liberate them. What we are seeing in the United States is an indication, if not proof, that at the higher technological levels industrialism can provide the abundance that once seemed a utopian pipe dream, and that on this abundance can be built a civilization in which opportunity is almost universal and special privilege at a minimum. If this is the direction in which the world is moving, there is little occasion for pessimism.

Certainly few of my Roxborough neighbors seem dissatisfied with their lot. They know, to be sure, that they're not living in Paradise: they and their families suffer from disease and accident; husbands and wives sometimes get along badly, and children are often a problem; no day is without its worries and irritations. But this is the kind of society they want to live in—one in which jobs are plentiful and pay is good and there are lots of things you can buy with your money. Their outlook on life may be materialistic, as some Europeans charge, but they are more easy-going about money than most Europeans of any nation or any class. They enjoy being generous and unsuspicious in money matters, and there are few of them who would cheat you unless they thought you were getting ready to cheat them. It would be reckless to say that all spend their money wisely, but most of them get what is for them their money's worth.

Whatever their personal problems, there are only two social problems that concern them, but these concern them constantly and deeply: the possibility of depression and the possibility of war. Either, they fully realize, can destroy most of what they value in life. Depression is something most of those over twenty-five know something about at first hand, for deprivation and fear in the early thirties left their mark even on the very young. As for war, it was less than a decade ago that atom bombs fell on Hiroshima and Nagasaki, and I think there are few of my neighbors who do not give daily thought to the chance of their falling on New York or Washington or Schenectady.

All America, of course, is in the same boat: either depression or war would be the end of the particular chapter we as a people are now writing. Since we have no assurance that we can avoid a depression and are even more dubious about preventing war, we can only regard our experiment thus far as tentative. But it is not any the less significant because it may be interrupted, or, for that matter, finished for good and all.

Even if we leave depression and war out of account, we know that we pay a price for what we have, but most of my neighbors would say it is not too high a price, and I feel that they are right. The price is to be defined chiefly in terms of the stresses and strains that are incident to the functioning of the great society. These stresses and strains are most palpable when you have to travel from Astor Place, say, to 125th Street on New York City's Lexington Avenue subway at five-thirty in an August heat wave, or when, in a November ice storm, you drive from a factory in the southeast section of Detroit to a housing project on the northwest boundary. Who can reckon the price in irritation and frustration, to say nothing of the threat to life and limb, that is paid by each one of millions of commuters in an age in which home is here and work is there? How many traumas, to say nothing of the accidents that get into the papers, are sustained in taking city and suburban families for a Sunday at the beach or in the country? It is no wonder that the people of the great society occasionally go berserk. The use of that phrase, however, borrowed as it is from a primitive society, reminds us that we are not the first human beings to live under a strain. If Freud is to be believed, the earliest stages of what we know as civilization had the greatest traumatic effects. And anyway, most of my neighbors would say, we are tough; we can take it.

The great society is necessarily a highly organized society, and organization is painful even when it is efficient, and doubly so when it isn't. The "hurry up and wait" of the war is constantly reflected in civilian life. The instrument of organization is bureaucracy, and the *sine qua non* of bureaucracy is red tape. One of my neighbors, who has driven his own express truck for more than thirty years, comments bitterly on the state regulations, ever more numerous and more com-

plicated, that apply to his business. He by no means believes
that all these regulations are unnecessary, but necessary or not,
they are annoying. The blunders of bureaucracy, whether the
United States Government's or Montgomery Ward's, are one
of the favorite topics of conversation in Roxborough.

Our version of the great society operates partly through
legal compulsions, partly through economic inducements, and
partly through persuasion. Persuasion most commonly takes
the form of advertising, and the advertising man is one of the
distinctive products of our culture. Since mass production is
possible only if a lot of people can be counted on to want the
same thing at the same time, some form of advertising is indispensable, but the constant assault to which our sensibilities
are subjected seems excessive. Fortunately most people develop an immunity to pressure and a skepticism regarding
claims, but the atmosphere is polluted just the same.

The truth is that the operation of the great society encourages the development of many unlovely characteristics.
Whether in government or in private business, the competi-
tion for power and prestige is intense, and the qualities that
make for success are not the finest mankind has known, as
American literature has been testifying for a long time. At the
turn of the century it was the businessman as robber baron,
as predator, that engaged the attention of our novelists. Then,
with Sinclair Lewis's *Babbitt,* we were shown the businessman
as Philistine. Today there is an increasing tendency to present
the businessman as a victim of the system by which we all live.
Such a novel as Cameron Hawley's *Executive Suite,* which in
its assumptions is friendly to business, exposes the brutality
of the struggle for power. Allan Seager's *Amos Berry* shows

power and creativity as antithetical. In government as in business, it is not social usefulness, but, all too often, a knife in some other man's back, that leads to power.

But the struggle for power was not an American invention, nor for that matter an invention of Western civilization, though Machiavelli was one of the first to codify the rules. For most of us it is lamentable that people should be corrupted by power, but what we are really concerned about is making sure that they don't have too much power over us, and in this respect we seem to be pretty successful. Our rough-and-ready democracy still knows how to cut a politician down to size, and today the biggest businessman cannot ignore the government or the unions.

What about the power we hold as a nation? It can be granted without argument that as a people we are not fit for the responsibilities that are now ours. What most of us wonder, however, with more humility than Comrade Vishinsky would give us credit for, is whether anybody else would do any better. For historical reasons, and not because of any particular virtue on our part, the modern revolution is farther advanced in this country than anywhere else and has shown clearer evidence of being a success. This at least suggests that we may have some qualifications for the tasks of leadership that have been laid upon us. If, to put it crudely, the world is going our way, it is not immodest of us to suppose that we may be able to give some good advice now and then.

The disparaging comments on American hegemony that come from so many Europeans seem a little unreasonable, for after all this was their revolution to begin with. The course of science, industry, democracy, and nationalism has been influenced by the geography of the North American continent, but one can understand these phenomena only in terms of the history of the Western world. We are, in short, part of Western civilization and that part of it in which its most characteristic tendencies have been most highly developed.

In Russia, as I have said earlier, the same forces are operating but under conditions vastly less favorable to their fruition. In combating Russian aggression, then, we are not only defending a kind of life that we find by and large to be good; we are also fighting to give the modern revolution its best chance of developing to the advantage of mankind.

XVI

Hope in America

Today there is so much that is encouraging in America, and the failure of Communism in Russia is so obvious, that I sometimes echo the question of my friend from the nearby town. "How did it happen," I ask myself, "that I fell for that gang?"

As I tried to show in the first part of this book, there is an answer. Those of us who became interested in Communism in the early thirties weren't wholly wrong, especially in our intentions. It was not wrong to try to act when millions of people were jobless and hungry. It was not wrong to want to abolish poverty and injustice. Up to a point and in a curious and highly qualified way I am proud of having been a Communist.

But history has long since made it clear to me that I bet on the wrong horse when I backed the Communist party. Whatever my intentions, my judgment couldn't have been worse. The mistake that I and so many others made in the thirties, it now seems to me, was in assuming that there must be *a* solution for the economic, political, and social problems created or made more urgent by the depression. Because of this we were suckers for Communism, which had everything figured out from the laws of history to the tactics of a hunger march. We were scornful of the experimental, piecemeal solutions of the New Deal; we wanted to have the whole mess cleaned up once and for all.

That is the kind of mistake that intellectuals are prone to make and, when I had finally come to terms with my decision to quit the party, I was determined not to be caught again in that particular trap. Today I regard with skepticism all dogmas—religious, social, political, or economic. I don't believe that there is a single cause for the present crisis, and I don't waste time looking for a simple solution. I don't believe that the world can be saved by a return to religion or a return to laissez faire, by a return to anything or an advance to anything that can be given an easy label. We have to work out our salvation as we go along, and we can count on making plenty of mistakes in the process.

I also decided that I would be better occupied with jobs that lay close at hand than with grandiose programs for remaking society, and ever since that time I have applied myself to the problems of Roxborough—fire protection, schools, library, and the like. As I said a few years ago in *Small Town*, I think it is healthy for the intellectual to break out of the isolation that seems in our society to be his fate. I am not, however, making a dogma of this; I am not leading a crusade back to the small towns; I am merely saying that it works for me. On the one hand, I take satisfaction in doing work whose results, however small, can be measured. And, on the other, I have acquired a somewhat different standard of values. If I am less scornful than are some intellectuals of the gadgets developed in the later stages of the industrial revolution, it is because I am benefiting by these gadgets, just as my neighbors are. In one large area of my life my values are identical with my neighbors' values, and I am not sorry that this is so.

That raises a large question: should the intellectual be a conformist? Only, I would say, to the extent that he can accept without damage to his conscience the values of the society he lives in. I don't believe in dissent for dissent's sake; it is the curse of the isolated urban intellectuals. But I believe even less in conformity for conformity's sake, or for the sake of money or power or prestige. As I have tried to say before, the health of society depends on the existence of free and vigorous criticism, and that is why the intellectuals as a class ought to be tolerated and perhaps even encouraged. Most of us have had the experience, while doing some little job around the house or on the car, of being completely baffled by a problem for which there seems to be no solution. Then somebody comes along and without any difficulty puts his finger on the right answer, not because he knows more than we do but because, being detached from the job and approaching it from a fresh point of view, he sees what we, in our closeness to it, have overlooked. That is the sort of thing that the intellectual is supposed to do with regard to the problems of society—and fairly often does.

But if we ought to tolerate any kind of criticism, we cannot afford to be undiscriminating. Those critics—and, as I have pointed out, there are still a few of them—who ignore the tyrannical and aggressive character of the Russian regime need not be listened to very attentively. Nor would I, for my own part, be much concerned with intellectuals who are so alienated from American society that they cannot recognize the great changes that have taken place in the past two decades.

Criticism that rests on private fantasies may sometimes be stimulating, but it isn't a dependable guide.

When my neighbors ask me what my political position now is, I explain that I am an independent voter, usually supporting Democratic candidates for national office but frequently voting Republican in local elections. Beyond that, I say, I am a liberal. That means, as I see it, that I am not committed to things as they are or things as they have been but am willing to examine freely proposals for change. It means also that, while recognizing the fallibility of the human reason, I believe that reason is what we chiefly have to rely on. There are no panaceas, no formulas, no short cuts; our situation has to be constantly scrutinized with all the intelligence we possess.

Liberalism is a term that has been badly abused, and therefore I am inclined to define my own position more sharply by calling it critical liberalism. Thus I distinguish it not only from Fake and Retarded Liberalism but also from what is sometimes described as ritualistic liberalism. The ritualistic liberal, who may or may not be retarded, has developed a pattern of automatic responses. The critical liberal, on the contrary, tries to analyze and deal with concrete situations. He knows that any situation may be full of contradictions, and that if the contradictions cannot be resolved they have to be lived with; they cannot be done away with by the use of a pat phrase. He is not dismayed if he discovers on occasion that he is in agreement with conservatives, and he doesn't feel that he always has to be on the unpopular side. He realizes that his view of the world is narrow, biased, inadequate, but he does as well as he can with what he has.

This is a rather abstract and idealized description of the

point of view from which I have tried to write this book. It will be clear from all I have said that I do not underestimate the importance of the struggle between what America represents in the world today and what Communist Russia represents, but I have no sympathy with the dogmatic anti-Communism that is so common in our country. In so far as communism is a body of ideas, it can be dealt with by analysis and argument; laws and investigations are as unnecessary as they are dangerous. On the other hand, Communist activity in the service of Russian aggression must be curbed, and I have no doubt that this can be done, if it is done calmly, without any infringement of our rights as citizens.

During the months in which I have been writing the book the dangers of dogmatic anti-Communism have become more and more apparent. When you live in a small town, you know that politics is a tough game, and you cease to be surprised by dirty tackles and the occasional use of brass knuckles. On the national, as on the local, scene neither party has hands clean enough to brag about. But it is impossible not to be disturbed when the leaders of the party in power deliberately adopt, for the sake of political advantage, the tactics of a Joe McCarthy. The Senator has shown himself as indifferent to the rights of citizens as he is to ordinary standards of truth and decency, and one sees an appalling possibility that the administration may follow him in this respect as it has in others. Although I have believed all along in attacking McCarthyism whenever I had a chance, I have refused to be an alarmist. It was a danger, I have said, but a danger that could be combated. I still believe that, but the fight is going to be nasty and some heads are going to be cracked in the course of it.

One of the worst things about dogmatic anti-Communism, aside from its threat to civil liberties, is the way it misleads its adherents. Every time a Communist loses his job or goes to jail, a certain section of the press hails a great victory for America, whereas it should be obvious that Russia has not been weakened in the slightest. Our war against Russia is being waged on a global scale, and we ought to be thinking in terms of perfecting our defenses, strengthening our allies, winning support within the Soviet Union and the satellites. We ought to be preparing ourselves for the sacrifices we shall have to make if the cold war continues and the infinitely greater sacrifices that will be necessary if the cold war becomes hot. If every Communist in America were to be converted or liquidated or otherwise disposed of tomorrow, the bigger part of our problem would still remain.

Dogmatic anti-Communism makes Russia seem stronger and the United States weaker than is actually the case. We are strong because we have come reasonably close to doing what Russia, in spite of all its promises, has failed to do: we have made industrialism serve the interests of all—or almost all—the people. I don't believe that American civilization is perfect, but I do maintain that this is the country in which the revolution of our times is most advanced, in which general prosperity and economic equality are somewhere near realization. If we use our strength wisely, we can win the war, cold or hot.

I like America and believe it is the hope of the world, but I do not think that Americans are better than other people, or that the United States is always right and other nations always wrong. I can understand why some countries, though no friendlier to Russia than we are, view our policies with distrust. We shall need more wisdom and more humility than we have generally shown as a nation if we are to overcome the suspicions of those who should be our allies. Much of the time we vacillate between smugness and a state bordering on hysteria. At one moment we are completely wrapped up in the pleasant distractions provided by our prosperity, and the next moment we are clamoring to put somebody or other in jail or maybe the electric chair. Yet it cannot be denied that so far we have come through our major tests pretty well. We have made the sacrifices that have been necessary to check Soviet aggression, and if the fabric of our democracy shows some worn spots here and there, it is still intact.

My neighbors know that, so far as community projects are concerned, I am a good deal of an optimist. I am rarely counted with those who shake their heads and say that this or that can't be done. The more you work with people, the more you realize that they are unpredictable. A few are pretty bad most of the time and a few are pretty good most of the time, but most people are always turning out to be a great deal worse and a great deal better than you expect them to be. There is so much inefficiency and irresponsibility, so much malice, so much laziness, that you don't see how anything can possibly be accomplished, and yet somehow, in spite of everything, things get done. One of the old standbys does a heroic job; somebody you hadn't counted on gives a boost; waning enthusiasm suddenly revives—and you have your new school building or your fire truck or whatever it is you want.

What I have seen in Roxborough convinces me that the modern revolution can be made to serve man and that man can, after a fashion, adapt himself to the revolution. It may be a long time before we are out of the shadow of impending catastrophe, and there will never be a day when the last of our problems is solved. But I believe that we shall pull through, as mankind always has, by the skin of our teeth, constantly going on from problem to problem, losing a little here, gaining a little there. All our intelligence and courage and good will will be terribly tested, but I believe that we have a fighting chance, and I don't know that we can expect more than that.